ADELPHI

PAPER·285

CONTENTS

Stability and Instability in Eastern Europe

PROFESSOR PETER FRANK

Here (in the Soviet Union) one can change the form of power only by changing society as a whole; or, to be more precise, by destroying the country and building a society of another type from its ruins.

The Reality of Communism (1981)
ALEXANDER ZINOVIEV

The region known as Central and Eastern Europe is sandwiched between Germany in the west and Russia in the east. When both powers are stable, and relations between them amicable, the chances of stability in the countries in between will also be good. Conversely, were both Russia and Germany to destabilise at the same time, it would almost certainly impose intolerable strain upon the rest of the region. At present Germany appears to have entered a period of low-level crisis, while Russia is in a seriously unstable condition. The prospects for the immediate future seem to be that Germany will remain more or less as it is (with the possibility of further, but not acute, deterioration), while the situation in Russia could spin out of control. The prognosis in the short to medium term, therefore, must be that the chances of instability in the region range from relatively low in the west to quite high in the east, but with the possibility of a knock-on effect generated by serious turbulence in Russia and the former Soviet Union that could impose severe strain on the whole of the continent east of the Elbe.

Germany is currently preoccupied with the reintegration of the former German Democratic Republic, whose costs (both economic and political) are proving to be much greater than at first envisaged. Nonetheless, the difficulties and strains that are being experienced are likely to be relatively short-term and, once the process has been completed, a larger, stronger, more assertive Germany will emerge that will doubtless be determined to play an extremely active role in the region, in Europe more broadly, and in the international realm as a whole.

At present, Germany's domestic circumstances are creating unfavourable reactions in the countries to the east, but to a degree that, so far, is tolerable. Economic recession is making German businesses more cautious about venturing capital investment in what is seen to be a high-risk area, while at the same time reducing the market potential for commodities and manufactures originating in the former socialist states (thus causing negative reactions in those countries attempting to self-finance their industrial recovery and accelerate the process of conversion of defence enterprises to civilian production).

The resurgence of right-wing extremism in Germany and the growing incidence of racist violence are also matters for concern, especially to countries that were victims of Nazism. Similarly, new, restrictive immigration laws are having an adverse impact upon neighbouring states to the east: as non-repressive receiving countries of first instance, they are having the problem of whether or not to accord asylum shifted back to them (and although Germany is providing financial assistance, any major influx of refugees, particularly from the former Soviet Union, would impose intolerable burdens upon the newly emancipated countries of Central Europe). Another disturbing factor is the irredentism that appears to be becoming more articulate and insistent in certain circles in Germany. At present, it relates mainly to the Sudetenland and to Silesia (and could, therefore, if it grew, complicate relations with the Czech Republic and Poland). There is the possibility, too, that irredentist clamour could extend to include Russia's anomalous enclave, Kaliningrad (formerly Königsberg). Such problems apart, however, Germany's influence on the region at present remains predominantly on the side of stability.

The same cannot be said of the former Soviet Union. Russia is in a state of acute crisis – economic, political, constitutional, social and, not least, moral. This is not surprising, since it is attempting to make an unprecedented transition from Soviet-type totalitarianism to some kind of vaguely pluralistic system, whose contours are only faintly discernible and whose route is utterly uncharted. While it is extremely unlikely that Russia will revert to its Soviet self, it is by no means certain that, in the foreseeable future, it will be transformed into a society that is economically liberal and politically democratic.

The main destabilising factor is the war of attrition that is taking place between the three branches of government. The legislative power (parliament, in the shape of the Supreme Soviet and the larger Congress of People's Deputies) is locked in a battle for state power with the executive (president and cabinet), while the judiciary (Constitutional Court), although claiming impartiality, is inclined to favour parliament.

The crux of the problem is the Constitution, which was adopted in 1978 when Brezhnevism was at its height. At that time, the Soviets (including the Supreme Soviet) served as a propagandistic façade behind which the Communist Party (CPSU) operated and in whose topmost organs political power was concentrated. Article 104 of the Constitution, which stated that parliament had supreme authority in all

matters, was a dead letter. But when the CPSU was disbanded following the abortive coup of August 1991, and with the demise of the
USSR as a state at the end of that year, Article 104 acquired substan-
tive meaning and, for the first time in its entire existence, the Russian
Supreme Soviet was infused with real power. It meant, too, that a
country embarking upon an unprecedented transition to democracy
was left saddled with what was (and remains) an essentially totalitarian constitution.

Since then, a stalemate has developed between the legislature and
the executive: parliament is invested with apparently unlimited power,
yet has few formal responsibilities; whereas the government is charged
with responsibility for virtually everything, but lacks the clout to carry
out its duties. Consequently, instead of the organs of government
attempting to resolve the serious crisis that besets Russia, immense
time and effort are expended in wasteful and destructive rivalry. It is
this issue (about which more will be said later) that is the main internal
destabilising factor and the one that exacerbates all other problems,
including that of foreign relations. A brief analysis of the conflicts that
arose in summer 1993 may serve to illustrate the damaging effects of
the 'dual power' (*dvoevlastie*) (or, as Trotsky would doubtless have
termed it, 'dual powerlessness') from which Russia is suffering.

Following President Boris Yeltsin's remarkable moral victory in the
April 1993 referendum (the results had no formal, constitutional validity) there were tentative signs that the tide was at last beginning to turn
in favour of reform. The rate of decline in production appeared to be
slowing down; the value of the rouble stabilised and even began to
strengthen against the US dollar. Crucially, in May, the government
and the Central Bank reached an informal agreement to limit credit,
followed later by the imposition of a real annual discount rate of
around 400%, only a little less than the then actual rate of inflation,
which was slowing down from 25% a month to some 15–10%. At
about the same time, coal prices were liberalised, with the likelihood
of knock-on effects on other basic industries such as steel production.
For the first summer in three years, free-market prices of fresh foods
were not rising. Hard currency reserves had accumulated to such an
extent that it was reported that each rouble in circulation was three-
quarters covered. Psychologically important, too, was the sustained
extension of privatisation and the consequential improvement in the
exchange value of the privatisation vouchers that all citizens had
received. Forecasts for the forthcoming harvest were optimistic. On
the non-economic front, the battle between executive and legislature,
although extremely bitter, continued to take the form of 'jaw' not war:
oft-predicted civil conflict had mercifully not erupted. In short, by

mid-1993 Russia was still in a state of acute crisis, but there were hesitant, encouraging signs that the decline had been arrested and that a slow, painful recovery might be in prospect.

The parliamentary opposition has no coherent political or economic programme. It uses its considerable power to obstruct, obfuscate and sabotage. Good news for the government is also bad news for it. It was very unwise, therefore, for President Yeltsin to choose such a moment to take a holiday and leave Moscow – he would have been better advised to have waited another couple of weeks until the Supreme Soviet had recessed for its summer break. The parliamentary speaker, Rhuslan Khasbulatov, seized the opportunity presented by Yeltsin's absence and struck.

First, the Supreme Soviet put a block on the presidential decree 'On guarantees of the right of citizens of Russia to participate in privatisation' and resolved to abolish the State Property Commission, the body responsible for selling off state assets (although deputies took good care to vote themselves the right to purchase at nominal cost their own accommodation both in Moscow and in their constituencies). The value of privatisation vouchers fell, as did confidence in the privatisation programme.

Then, on 22 July, without consulting the Ministry of Finance, parliament approved a budget for 1993 which, if implemented, would produce a deficit over the year of some 15–25% of gross national product, far in excess of the government's own intended 10% deficit. As David Dyker has observed, if this were to go ahead, any idea of macrostabilisation of the economy would be 'illusory'.

With these two moves, the parliamentary opposition succeeded in exposing the extreme fragility of the political process in Russia. In a matter of days, the mood changed from cautious optimism to one of acute crisis, anxiety and even fear. Khasbulatov announced that the Presidium of the Supreme Soviet would remain in session throughout the summer break (and in fact deputies were recalled to Moscow soon after): 'Sharp turns of events cannot be ruled out and we must maintain an organising centre'. In similar vein, a leader of the Democratic Russia movement, Lev Ponomaryov, warned of the possibility of another coup, while *Izvestiya*, a pro-government newspaper, reproached Yeltsin in a headline that read: 'When democracy is under threat Russia must hear the voice of its president'. At this, Yeltsin, broke off his vacation and returned to the capital. Thus was optimism transformed into pessimism and apparent stability into incipient instability in just a few days. Once again, the inherent weakness in Russia had proved to be the inappropriateness of its constitution and, stemming from that, the unsuitability of its institutional structures to the task of democratic transformation.

The problem was not new: Central and Eastern Europe had undergone much the same experience. But there was a clearer awareness of the nature of the problem and what to do about it. Leaders such as President Vaclav Havel of Czechoslovakia had soon realised that democracy does not follow automatically when communism collapses: 'We have done away with the totalitarian system, but we have yet to win democracy', he pointed out. It was a sentiment echoed by Adam Michnik, the Polish historian, Solidarity activist and newspaper editor, when he remarked at a conference in Vienna in February 1991, six months before the coup in Russia, that:

> In all these countries [of Central and Eastern Europe] dictatorship has lost and freedom has won. But that does not mean that democracy has won. Democracy means the institutionalisation of freedom. We do not yet have a democratic order and that is why our freedom is so fragile and shaky.

As a first step following the revolutions of 1989, constitutions were replaced or amended and/or new parliamentary elections held. Only in Russia was the old institutional structure left in place, thus creating a source of permanent instability.

The Union of Soviet Socialist Republics was an intrinsically ersatz creation founded on violence and maintained by fear. Once the CPSU was suppressed, it was just a matter of time before the Union disintegrated, too. When it did, the break-up posed numerous delicate questions about the relationship between the heartland of the former imperial power, Russia, and the newly independent republics (both those within the Commonwealth of Independent States (CIS) and those without).

The dismantling of the Soviet Union was a precipitate act. Its purpose was to complete the destruction of the unified CPSU to get rid of Gorbachev. But in their haste to be done with the old system, the leaders of the new states created problems of a different kind. Now that there was an army without a state, to whom should it swear its allegiance? Who was to police frontiers? How was trade to be conducted, and in what currency? How were laws to be harmonised, if at all?

Since the end of 1991, the successor states to the USSR have, in the circumstances, coped with these particular problems better than might have been expected. But independence has also brought in its wake serious instability on the periphery of the former Union and, in certain cases, between and within individual countries: for example, the prob-

lem of relations between Russians and the name nationalities of Estonia, Latvia and Lithuania; internal strife in Moldova and the involvement of the Russian 14th Army commanded by General Aleksandr
Lebed in the self-proclaimed Trans-Dniestr republic; tensions between
Russia and Ukraine over the control of strategic nuclear weaponry; and
a serious dispute concerning the division of the Black Sea Fleet and the
naval base at Sevastopol, not to mention the question of the Crimean
peninsula itself. (It remains to be seen whether or not the agreements
concluded between presidents Yeltsin and Kravchuk at Massandra on
3 September 1993 are ratified by the parliaments of Russia and
Ukraine.) The Caucasus are once again in a state of war, with Russian
troops allegedly embroiled in the conflict between Georgia and
Abkhazia. Still in the Caucasus, but this time within the Russian
Federation itself, North Ossetia, Ingushetia and Chechnia are experiencing varying degrees of turbulence; while the Nagorno-Karabakh
issue has escalated into *de facto* war between Armenia and Azerbaijan
(itself in a state of near civil war).

The violence in Tajikistan (at times comparable in its intensity and
cruelty to what is happening in the former Yugoslavia), together with
the grave situation on the Tajikistan–Afghanistan frontier, may be a
foretaste of things to come elsewhere in Central Asia. The five countries of that area – Turkmenistan, Uzbekistan, Kyrgyzstan, Tajikistan
and parts of Kazakhstan – formerly constituted the region known very
generally as Turkestan. There, the idea of the nation-state is weakly
developed: when in 1924, for example, people in that region were
asked in a survey to identify themselves according to their nationality,
the majority replied simply: 'Musselman'. Not only is the region
actually or incipiently unstable, it is seen by Russia as a possible
'launching pad' for Islamic fundamentalism (such is Russian paranoia
about Islam that any Muslim who manifests political behaviour not in
accord with Russian interests is dubbed automatically 'fundamentalist', 'militant' or 'extremist').

The relevance of the situation in the Caucasus and Central Asia to
the question of stability or instability in Europe lies partly in the
destabilising effects that would probably occur if very large numbers
of Russian expatriates were to return to the heartland in disorganised
panic. To some extent, this is happening already, thus imposing severe
strain on the social infrastructure and contributing to the general at-
mosphere of political volatility in Russia. But there could be even
more serious consequences; at least, that is the view of the Russian
Deputy Minister for Foreign Affairs with special responsibility for
Asian and Central Asian questions, Georgii Kunadze.

The overriding concern, according to Kunadze, is to ensure that Islamic extremism does not penetrate into Russia. Therefore, it is essential that there should be stability in and between the countries of the region, including economic stability, without which not only would the Russian-speaking population be put at risk, but so also would Russia's internal economic reform programme (because of the effect that regional economic instability could have upon the rouble). Moreover, Kunadze argues, the Tajikistan–Afghanistan frontier is a little over 1,300 kilometres in length. Were Russia to withdraw from the region entirely, there would be the problem of guarding a Russia–Kazakhstan border 6,000km long: 'This is not just a line on a map, but an engineering-construction system costing a very great deal of money. If we withdraw from this frontier [Tajikistan–Afghanistan], then we must decide where and when we shall build a new frontier'.

Kunadze's main concern, however, is not just logistical and financial, for he goes on to say:

> Obviously, not one of the countries of Central Asia is capable without our help of protecting its own borders. We have run up against this problem in Tajikistan. If we were to leave, we must be prepared for Islamic extremism, for the forces of instability in general, to pass through Tajikistan, enter Kyrgyzstan, and from there it is not far to Kazakhstan, before these forces are on the threshold of Russia.

Pursuing this line of analysis a stage further Kunadze even envisages the possibility of the formation of new states, in particular a new Islamic republic made up of the southern provinces of Tajikistan and the northern provinces of Afghanistan. What he does not refer to explicitly, but which may have been at the back of his mind, is the possibility of internal instability in Kazakhstan (although unconfirmed rumour suggests that with the rise of national consciousness in Kazakhstan and the uncertainty surrounding Kazakhstan's predominantly Russian-settled northern oblasts, this republic is now the cause of extreme anxiety in Moscow).

The general hypothesis of this paper is that Russia is the key to stability in Central and Eastern Europe. It follows, therefore, that the wider the concentric circles of instability, the greater the likelihood of crisis spreading beyond Russia's borders. At the heart of the matter is the problem of constitutionality, of statehood (*gosudarstvennost*). Moving outwards from the centre, there is the problem of Russia's relations with its erstwhile fellow republics and, finally, the question of safeguarding its borders, be they at the limits of the Federation or beyond. There is, however, a wider – world – context in which the plight of Russia can be set.

In summer 1993 the journal *Foreign Affairs* published a remarkably original and stimulating article by Professor Samuel P. Huntington entitled 'The Clash of Civilisations?'. In it, he argues that:

> The fundamental source of conflict in [the] new world will not be primarily ideological or primarily economic. The great divisions among humankind and the dominating source of conflict will be cultural. Nation states will remain the most powerful actors in world affairs, but the principal conflicts of global politics will occur between nations and groups of different civilisations. The clash of civilisations will dominate global politics. The fault lines between civilisations will be the battle lines of the future.

Professor Huntington identifies eight major civilisations: Western, Confucian, Japanese, Islamic, Hindu, Slavic-Orthodox, Latin-American and African. He stresses that differences do not necessarily mean conflict, but he does point out that, over the centuries, differences among civilisations 'have generated the most prolonged and the most violent conflict'.

With the end of the Cold War, the fault line between Western Christianity and Orthodox Christianity and Islam in Europe has replaced the former ideological boundary (witness in particular the current Balkan conflict). Thus, in a sense, the division of Europe has moved eastwards. The implications for Russia, still further east of that imaginary line, are potentially even more profound.

The Russian Federation (Slavic-Orthodox), or Russia in the shape of the defending force on the frontiers of neighbouring states, is at the interface of four out of the other seven civilisations. Implicit in Professor Huntington's argument is the assumption that the greater the number of fault lines a state touches upon, the greater the likelihood (although not inevitability) of conflict. Given that *within* the Russian Federation there are numerous relatively minor, but significant, internal fault lines (as evidenced by the tensions between Moscow and ethnic republics such as Chechnia, Sakha and Tatarstan), the probability of conflict is even further enhanced.

Similar strains may be observed in the countries of Central and Eastern Europe, either within-state or between states: Russians and Poles in the Baltics; Poles in Belarus and Ukraine; Russians and Gagauz in Moldova; and Russian-speaking eastern Ukraine. Further west there are problems associated with German minorities in Poland and the Czech Republic, and Hungarians in Romania, Slovakia and the former Yugoslavia, all of which are potential sources of instability. The one factor, however, that acts as a constraint upon these states (with, so far, the tragic exception of Yugoslavia) is that they all perceive themselves as being part of a broad European cultural tradition to which they hope to return. In many respects, as has been cogently argued by Thomas W. Simons, Jr, this perception is a myth. But, as he points out, myths can be very powerful and if this one is capable of encouraging self-restraint and the maintenance of peace in the region, good luck to it!

Russia, too, subscribes to the myth, but to a more limited and ambivalent degree. The debate between Westernisers and Slavophiles is as old as the Russian state itself and the present rivalry between the so-called nationalist hardliners and the Western-oriented democrat-marketeers is perhaps just the latest manifestation. It may, therefore, be significant that in political discourse in Russia the phrase that occurs more often than 'a return to Europe' is 'a return to civilisation' (although this begs the question, of course, of which civilisation that should be). In other words, the myth is probably of greater utility in Central and Eastern Europe than it is in Russia for, to paraphrase Marx, the further east one goes in Europe the weaker and less developed is democracy.

It is singularly unfortunate, and perhaps the greatest irony of the late twentieth century, that just at the moment when the newly self-liberated, former communist states are in need of a role model, the model that they prefer (and the one which throughout the Cold War they were exhorted to emulate), is itself undergoing a crisis of confidence and economic recession. From Britain in the north – where practically all the traditional main supports of society are exhibiting varying degrees of decrepitude – to Italy in the south, most of Western Europe is experiencing serious problems of one kind or another. Precisely at a time when some countries in the east are seeking ways to integrate their multinational populations, integration inside the European Community (EC) has entered a period of crisis. Similarly, just when Russia's southern rim is erupting into violence and is desperately in need of example, both the United Nations (UN) and the North Atlantic Treaty Organisation (NATO) states are apparently incapable of restoring order to the Balkans.

This is not to say that the West has ignored the plight of the former Soviet bloc; far from it. But welcome though aid in the form of credit, cash, foodstuffs, pharmaceuticals and know-how may be, the east has an even greater need for a role model, a model that exemplifies not only political structures and a market economy, but also such virtues as probity in public life and a general observance of legal and moral norms. Possibly the most pernicious legacy of communist rule is the cynicism, amorality, selfishness and disposition towards criminality that disfigure all the Central and Eastern European societies and, in particular, Russia and the rest of the former Soviet Union. Not only are these impediments to building a civil society regulated by the rule of law, they are also destabilising factors that could spill over national boundaries and pollute the rest of Europe.

Scarcity is a breeding ground for crime; so is the virtual absence of a clearly defined and determinedly enforced set of legal norms. In the former Soviet Union in particular, criminal groupings that existed in embryonic form under the old regime have been quick to organise themselves into extensive 'mafias' and to extend their activities into the realms of drug trafficking, illicit arms sales, smuggling and money laundering. Not only is this affecting the former communist states (Prague, for example, is now a major entrepot for drugs, many of which originate in, or are shipped via, Soviet Central Asia), it is penetrating Western Europe, too. The discovery by the British police of stocks of sophisticated hand weaponry suspected of having been smuggled in from Eastern Europe or Russia, the organised theft of computers in Britain (especially Apple Macintosh) for resale at phenomenally high prices in Russia, and the kidnapping and holding to ransom of a prominent Swedish businessman are but three recent examples of a growing lawlessness that is likely to increase rather than diminish so long as the former Soviet Union remains in crisis.

Other exportable sources of instability are environmental pollution, disease and nuclear catastrophe. Chernobyl was a terrifying reminder of the impossibility of confining the effects of nuclear accidents within national boundaries. What happened at Chernobyl was not so much technical failure or the consequence of poor design; it was the result primarily of human error caused by low levels of professional competence and general demoralisation. Nor is it obvious that the situation in this respect has changed for the better since 1986. Nuclear power stations (including in Ukraine) continue to give cause for acute concern. Any major accident (even, say, in the Caucasus, where it is proposed to reactivate the station near Yerevan) could have serious consequences for countries to the west, both in terms of pollution and the possible exodus of large numbers of refugees.

There is little wonder that with the country awash with seemingly intractable problems, with so many citizens suffering economic hardship, and at a time of escalating political crisis, the peoples of Russia yearn for stability, order, competence and professionalism in public life. It is dismaying for them to observe the unedifying and dangerous squabbling that increasingly substitutes for politics in Russia. Again, this is a consequence of the constitutional deadlock that exists between president and parliament; but it is at such times that the seductively simple solutions of demagogues may find a receptive audience, unless, that is, more sober, responsible leaders come to the fore.

With members of Yeltsin's circle locked in unseemly struggle with Vice-President Rutskoi and the parliamentary leadership (with charges and counter-charges of corruption serving as a surrogate for politics), it is noticeable that the prime minister, Viktor Chernomyrdin, is unobtrusively gaining ground on both parties and beginning to impress with his quiet purposefulness. His credentials as a reformer are scant and his political preferences opaque, but he seems to have realised that the country cannot be saved by a reversion to hypercentralised economic planning and profligate allocations of credit to loss-making industrial enterprises. At the same time, he appears to be at least doing *something*, while his relations with the prime ministers of Ukraine and Belarus offer the prospect of some kind of economic union between the three Slav states that could in turn have a calming, stabilising effect on the rest of Eastern Europe.

This paper has focused upon Russia partly because that country is the author's main area of expertise, but, more particularly, as was argued at the outset, because Russia holds the key to stability in Central and Eastern Europe.

Stability in Russia is not in itself a guarantee of stability elsewhere. But there is little doubt that, were Russia to degenerate into violent disorder, economic breakdown or environmental catastrophe, it would have extremely serious adverse consequences for Central and Eastern Europe, too. Moreover, there are several issues that could give rise to serious conflict between the former communist states, particularly involving territorial or ethnic issues. At the same time, the aspiring democracies are experiencing varying degrees of economic difficulty. Poland, Hungary and the Czech Republic are performing comparatively successfully and therefore have better prospects for internal stability than have, say, Slovakia and Romania. Overall, however, Central and Eastern Europe have chosen to turn their face Westwards; they see themselves as part of a wider Europe, a Europe that subscribes to the values of Western liberal democracy and the free market. Only Russia is ambivalent and unsure about whether or not it wishes to espouse the Western European tradition, be 'Atlanticist', a Euro-Asian power or, characteristically, find its own unique destiny. Much will depend upon the outcome of the political struggle that is taking place. For all his imperfections – political and personal – Boris Yeltsin continues at present to offer the best prospects of a Westward-facing Russia. But should he be defeated, the chances are that he would be succeeded by someone more inward-looking, more authoritarian, more nationalistic and less disposed to cooperate with the West. *Pozhivem uvidim!* – We must wait and see!

Russia: Partner or Risk Factor in European Security?

PROFESSOR HANNES ADOMEIT

Introduction

Is Russia a partner or a risk factor in European security? At present it is more of the former than the latter, but will this continue to be true? Examining current Russian foreign policies and principles can provide only some of the answer. The main part lies in the country's internal evolution. This is, of course, not much different in other countries; international security policies always depend on domestic factors. What is different today in Russia is the country's instability and the broad spectrum of possible changes in foreign and security policy that could result from shifts in domestic affairs. This spectrum is governed by four major transformation processes: the transition from a command economy and state ownership to private property and the market; from an authoritarian or totalitarian one-party state to a pluralist democracy based on the rule of law; from a unitary, centralised state to a federation with power allocated not only to ethnically non-Russian titular entities, but also to Russian administrative units; and from imperial structures and consciousness to a more modest Russian identity.

It is difficult to rank the importance of these transformations in relation to each other and the conduct of foreign policy. The fourth transformation process, however, is probably the least autonomous; its direction and future shape critically depend on the first three. Hence, this paper discusses first the economic, political, military and federal problems and their impact on current security concepts and policies. Their interrelationship with, and effect on, the issue of a Russian national identity and national interests is discussed next, followed by an attempt to reconstruct the present Russian approach to European security issues. A final step examines how various lines of development are likely to impinge on future Russian security policies in Europe.

Economic transformations

The economic condition of Russia (it would seem) has improved from the abysmal to the merely dismal with a spectacular contraction in production. To give some idea of the scale involved, the fall in gross national product (GNP) in the United States during the Great Depression of 1932 was about 14%. In contrast, Soviet GNP in 1991 alone declined by 17%. In 1992, according to official figures, Russia's GNP shrunk by another 19% and industrial production by 24%. Even if recent Western calculations for a less marked decline in GNP in 1992 were to be accepted, the contraction from the base figures of 1990 would still be enormous by any measure of comparison.[1]

There has also been a sharp increase in the rate of inflation, which in 1992 stood at about 2,500%. Wage and salary increases could not keep pace with that rate of increase, which in turn produced drastic declines in real income for many people.[2] The sharp deterioration in the standard of living has had political consequences and has impeded rapid economic reform.

The high inflation rates have contributed to the precipitous fall in the value of the rouble. In the Soviet period, at official rates, 60 or 70 kopecks would buy one dollar; today, more than 1,000 roubles are needed. There is a wide discrepancy between the purchasing power of the rouble and exchange rates which has led to socially disruptive distortions. Today, a taxi driver will earn more money in a few hard-currency trips to Moscow-Sheremetevo airport in an afternoon than top nuclear scientists at the Kurchatov Institute or coal miners in Magadan earn in a month.

Some of the worst effects of the transition to the market are yet to come. In summer 1993 the proportion of unemployed was less than 1% of the total workforce. As large-scale inefficient enterprises are cut off from lavish subsidies, threatened by bankruptcy and workers made redundant, the number of unemployed – and the social malaise and misery – is bound to increase substantially.

The contraction of productive capacity, the collapse of the Council for Mutual Economic Assistance (CMEA), the disintegration of the Soviet arms industry and the decline in the world price for oil have had a devastating effect on Russia's foreign trade and its ability to pay its debts. The share of Russia in the world market has shrunk from about 4% in the Soviet period to perhaps only 1% at present.

Inflation is still a big problem. The monthly rate, which had been running at about 25% until February 1993, dropped to an encouraging 15% in the spring. However, relaxation of fiscal discipline and steep rises in electricity prices made the inflation rate jump to about 30% in August. This obviously has serious domestic repercussions; but it also affects Russia's ability to draw on several components of the Group of Seven's $43 billion assistance package, including the rescheduling of Russia's $80bn debt, a $6bn rouble stabilisation fund and $4.1bn in

International Monetary Fund (IMF) 'stand-by' loans. These and other international credits and assistance schemes are available only if a credible macroeconomic stabilisation programme can be put in place.

There are, however, some signs of economic progress. Capital flight has decreased and dollar deposits in Russian banks have grown to $14bn.[3] The rate of subsidisation of state enterprises has decreased. In 1992, central-bank credit issued to factories and other businesses totalled 26% of gross domestic product (GDP). In the second half of 1993, estimates are that the rate will be less than 10% of GDP.[4] The greatest success, however, has been evident in the sphere of privatisation. In the spring of 1992 small enterprises, such as shops and restaurants, were privatised. By the beginning of June 1993, 70,000 of these smaller businesses, or 54% of the total, had been converted to private ownership. The first auction at which a medium-sized business issued shares in exchange for privatisation vouchers took place in December 1992. Since then, progress has been spectacular. As Anatolii Chubais, the minister in charge of privatisation, reported, at the beginning of June 1993 half of the 9,000 medium- and large-size enterprises had been privatised through voucher auctions, including such giants as ZIL – the maker of limousines for the Kremlin elite – and Uralmash, Russia's largest maker of machine tools. This meant that about one-third of the workforce in industry was no longer working in the state sector.[5]

Political transformations
There are definite signs of political stabilisation even though democratisation may be one of its victims. After the failed coup in August 1991, Boris Yeltsin missed an important opportunity by failing to call for the immediate dissolution of the Congress of People's Deputies (CPD) and new parliamentary elections. As a result, conservative and right-wing forces were able to stage a come-back. Their influence reached its peak and governmental authority its lowest point in the period from December 1992 to March 1993 when the CPD forced the removal of Prime Minister Gaidar from office, blocked reformist measures and aimed Russian foreign policy in a more assertive, self-centred direction. A *théâtre absurd* ensued, with the parliaments, the executive and the Supreme Court all accusing each other of violating the Soviet-era constitution and its 300-plus subsequent amendments. In a perversion of checks and balances, the branches of government had sufficient power to obstruct each other, but not enough to devise and implement coherent policies. The fate of reform hung in the balance, and Yeltsin himself barely avoided impeachment.

The 25 April referendum was the first important turning point in the political struggle. Prior to the referendum, there were widespread fears that electoral participation would be low; that many regions would fail to carry it out or make a mockery of it by adding their own questions; that it would be meaningless because of its consultative rather than binding quality; and that it would be ambiguous because a plurality of voters would probably express confidence in the president (question 1), but reject the social and economic policies conducted by him and the government since 1992 (question 2).

None of these concerns turned out to be warranted and the turnout was quite large (about 65.7%). Yeltsin not only won the confidence of 59.2% of the voters, but 53.6% also supported his programme of economic change. While more than two-thirds of the voters supported new elections for parliament, less than half called for presidential elections. Backed by a popular mandate Yeltsin went on the offensive, attempting to rein in the CPD and the parliament and calling on Russia's regions to send two delegates each to a constituent assembly to draft a new constitution.

Yeltsin continued his political offensive in autumn 1993. The day before parliament planned to pass a budget that Yeltsin had twice vetoed, and which, if implemented, would have driven the country into hyperinflation, he disbanded that body and called for new elections on 11–12 December. He also advised the constitutional court not to convene prior to that date and placed the central bank under direct control of the government. The culmination of the conflict came on 3–4 October, when parliamentary leaders, their counter-president and allies from the 'red–brown' camp made a crucial miscalculation by ordering an attack on the Ostankino television complex, the mayor's office and the Kremlin. The balance of political and security forces overwhelmingly favoured the president who, after using force against the opposition, found himself in a commanding position.

Yeltsin's victory is not complete, either in Moscow or the country as a whole. However, he now has the chance, if he wants to use it, to implement more comprehensive reform measures and impose vitally necessary fiscal discipline. Crises and political struggles at the top will undoubtedly continue. There is also no point in idealising Yeltsin as a liberal democrat, which he is not. But thus far he has been willing to promote reform against parliamentary and regional obstructionism, and in this endeavour his hand has been strengthened.

Military transformations
In the military realm, too, there are some tendencies towards stabilisation. The height of the armed forces' demoralisation was ap-

parently reached in late 1992 and early 1993. Several shocks and setbacks had taken their toll, including the withdrawal or ousting of combat forces and advisers from all corners of the globe; the collapse of empire and union; large-scale destruction of military equipment as required by the Intermediate-range Nuclear Forces (INF) and Conventional Armed Forces in Europe (CFE) treaties; conflicting claims in the successor states on the loyalty of the forces stationed on their territory; and controversies over the disposition of equipment (e.g., the Black Sea Fleet, conventional forces and nuclear weapons). Military morale had also deteriorated because of extensive budgetary cuts, a falling standard of living, a severe shortage of housing, internal corruption and low social esteem for the military profession.

These problems were highlighted by extensive draft evasion. In early 1993, about 60% of draft-age Russians failed to report for service.[6] Draft evasion and liberal deferment laws meant that, in the spring of 1993, less than 300,000 (16.5%) out of a total of about two million men eligible for the draft were likely to be called up. Most units of the Russian armed forces were at best about 30–40% of normal strength.[7]

In 1992 doubts were justified as to whether integrity of command still existed. There were several instances of the involvement of Russian armed forces in the geopolitical space of the former Soviet Union (see below). But in each and every case it was unclear to the outside observer who was responsible for intervention: whether it was the political leadership in Moscow; the top military leadership of the Russian armed forces or the joint military command of the Commonwealth of Independent States (CIS); the commander of the military districts (okrugi), for instance, the Transcaucasian or Baltic military districts; the commanders of individual armies or regiments, such as the 14th Army in Trans-Dniestr; or individual units and 'local heroes'.

The present military picture is different from that of 1992. The impression now is that the unity of command has been restored. Pavel Grachev himself, in a recent interview, was exuberant ('Thank God, the soul rejoices') about improved military morale and discipline, noting that on his visits to military districts he had encountered a new self-confidence and a new desire to serve.[8] But there are also new requirements to serve. In May 1993 parliament responded to previous complaints by the military leadership about draft evasion and deferments, and cancelled the draft deferment of those over 20 years of age who were entering institutions of higher education for the first time.[9] The reduction in the overall strength of the Russian armed forces from about 1.8 million officers and men at present to 1.45m will make the task of filling the ranks easier and enhance the prospects for a leaner, more efficient and more effective army.

But what about the role of the military in politics? On this issue it is useful to remember Foreign Minister Kozyrev's warning of the previous year that pressure for the Russian Army to intervene in support of ethnic Russians living outside Russia's borders, as in Moldova and South Ossetia, was being orchestrated by politicians opposed to Yeltsin. What was 'happening in Russia today' reminded him of the events in Germany in 1933, when 'democrats began to change over to nationalist positions'. He feared that in Russia, the 'party of war, the party of neo-Bolsheviks' was raising its head, 'using their supporters in the military to fan ethnic flames and then appealing to Russian patriotism'. For all these reasons there was the 'danger of an anti-democratic coup'.[10]

In 1993, the danger of a right-wing, anti-democratic coup did indeed exist. But it did not emanate from the military. The chiefs of the armed forces, police and internal security supported Yeltsin at the 9th CPD congress in March 1993. In the 25 April 1993 referendum, more than 65% of the military personnel voted for the President. At the June 1993 military conference in Moscow the military commanders endorsed his draft constitution;[11] and in the autumn confrontation with parliament Yeltsin retained the support of the three security ministries. His defence and security ministers were able to use elite units – the Taman and Kantemirov tank divisions, the Dzerzhinksy internal security division and airborne forces from Ryazan – to restore presidential control. None of the chief commanders of combat forces and military districts, as far as is known, came out in support of the opposition. They obviously knew better than to risk their careers by backing the losing side.

Yeltsin has played his cards right. He has been careful to court military support, involving Grachev in day-to-day decision-making on security- and foreign-policy matters, showing his concern for the officers' housing problems and granting frequent salary increases. As his defence minister gratefully acknowledged on this last issue: 'Today, they [officers, non-commissioned officers and men] finally receive pay on which not only they themselves are able to live, but also their families'.[12]

The strength, effectiveness and political loyalty of the Russian armed forces are also important factors in whether Russia is likely to break up or develop viable forms of federalism.

Russia: federalism or break-up?
The break-up of the Russian Federation would have profound repercussions on European security. Is Russia, then, to be compared to a doll within a doll (*matroyshka*), an empire within an empire, whose

inevitable fate is that of disintegration because it possesses the very same properties as its larger shell: the Soviet Union?

Russia, like the former USSR, is a multi-ethnic state no longer held together by Marxist–Leninist ideology and police repression. In many of the former Soviet republics and the Russian Federation, ideology has been replaced by ethnically based nationalism as a source of legitimacy. Nationalism in turn provides the driving force for independence movements and irredentism, sovereignty and separatism – and violent ethnic conflict.

All this can be regarded as the logical result of an imperialist political and economic system established in the Tsarist period and reconstituted under Stalin with an even greater degree of centralisation and repression. The Yeltsin government is now saddled with the problem of Stalin's *divide et impera* principle, having drawn the borders not only of the union republics, but also of the autonomous republics and regions in accordance with arbitrary political rather than ethnic criteria.

'Ethnic conflicts', however, are hardly ever simply ethnic. They are often supplemented and sometimes supplanted by religious fervour, struggles for political power and rivalry over economic resources. Indeed, many of the recent demands for sovereignty or 'special status' within the Federation are primarily economic and political rather than ethnic. This applies to the claims of such titular republics as Bashkiria (Bashkortostan) and Mari, and the Sverdlovsk, Vologda and Primorye administrative regions. All these areas have a disproportionately greater share of important natural resources or industrial assets over which they would like more control.

One of the vehicles for the assertion of regional economic interests has been the Constitutional Assembly with its 700 delegates from the 88 regions that still consider themselves part of the Federation. Called by Yeltsin in the spring of 1993 to codify a new distribution of power between the executive, legislative and judicial branches, the Assembly turned into a forum for debate about power-sharing between the centre and the regions. One of the paragraphs of the draft document described Russia's 21 ethnically defined republics as 'sovereign states' and called its 67 territorial–administrative regions 'formations within the state'. This has been regarded as unacceptable by several of the regions since they want the same economic and political rights as the republics. Such tendencies were evident also in Yeltsin's Federative Council. Both institutions, however, are now being bypassed by Yeltsin who has called for ratification of the constitution by referendum.

What is most important in the context of a discussion of federalism versus break-up, however, is the fact that claims for a greater degree of autonomy are not the same as demands for independence and separation from Russia. Furthermore, a good argument can be made that what is needed for the reconstruction of Russia and more rapid economic progress is delegation of power to the regions rather than continuation of centralisation. Conversely, the regions – both the ethnically defined and the territorial–administrative formations – may well conclude that economic and political interests could be advantageous or could even call for continued membership of the Russian Federation.

As for tendencies of the ethnically defined republics to separate from the Federation, there are several facts and factors which counteract such trends.[13] First, the proportion of non-Russians in the autonomous republics of the Russian Federation is only 17% as compared to 48% in the former USSR. Russians are in a minority only in Daghestan (which is multinational and has no 'titular' nation), Kabardino-Balkaria (binational), Chechnia (internally divided), Ingushetia (cooperating with Russia), North Ossetia (relying on Russia in the conflict with both Muslims and Georgians), Tatarstan, Kalmykhia and Tuva. Second, geography advises against separation since most of the autonomous regions are not located at the periphery, but in the midst of the Russian Federation. The North Caucasian republics, therefore, are a special case. Third, there is the problem of economic viability. Most of the republics and regions could not survive unless Russia were willing to grant transit rights. Fourth, unlike the ex-Soviet republics or Latvia, Lithuania, Estonia and Ukraine, the republics in the Russian Federation do not have any previous experience of state and nationhood. It would be rather artificial, and certainly very difficult, for them to construct a national consciousness.

The conclusion to be drawn from all these complex factors and contradictory trends is that it is far too simple to predict the fate of Russia by extrapolating from the collapse of the Soviet Union. There are important differences between the two cases.

Having reviewed the economic, political, military and federal dimensions of security policy, what then are the consequences for the definition of Russian identity and Russian national interests?

Russian national identity and national interests
Picking up the pieces in Russia itself and developing a sensible definition of Russian identity and Russian national interests is obviously difficult. First, apart from survival and territorial integrity there is nothing axiomatic or self-evident about any country's 'national interest'. National interests exist in the plural; they are related to group interests, which in turn have to be adjudicated by means of compro-

mise. This, however, is an idea that is yet to be grasped in the Russian debate.

Second, from the perspective of creating a Russian nation-state the current Russian boundaries make no sense. The Russian Federation as presently constituted is both too small and too large – too small because of the more than 25m Russians who live outside that state, and too large because of approximately the same number of non-Russians (17% of the population) who live within its confines.[14]

Third, the boundaries as well as the new independent states are artificial creations. As mentioned above, when the republics and autonomous regions were established by Stalin their viability and possible separation from the centre were to be ruled out rather than encouraged. Russians now confronted with the question of whether their national interests are best served by accepting unreservedly the independence of the new states in the 'near abroad' (as Russians incongruously call the geopolitical space of the former Soviet Union), or by attempting to re-establish indirect control much like the Western powers did in the Third World after decolonisation.

A fourth problem concerns the instruments of nation-building. It would be highly dangerous for Moscow to use Russian nationalism as a device by which to construct a separate national identity. The danger derives from the multi-ethnic character of Russia and the existence of Russian minorities outside Russia. Ethnic Russian assertiveness would undoubtedly exacerbate counter-nationalism(s) with disruptive if not disastrous consequences for the Russian Federation and the Russian minorities living in the 'near abroad'. Sensibly, therefore, the government has emphasised civic virtues rather than ethnicity in its approach to nation-building.

Finally, the initial idea behind the foundation of the CIS at the Brest fortress in early December 1991 was that of a Slavic Union, consisting of Russia, Belorussia (as it then was) and Ukraine. Even though the subsequent summit in Alma-Ata in late December 1991 broadened CIS membership, the fact remains that Russians have to decide whether their country is to have a more narrowly ethnic Russian identity, form part of a Slavic construction, emphasise Western European and Western values or revert to the idea of a special 'Eurasian' character and mission.

If a classification of the main orientations *en vogue* in Russia today were to be attempted, three major schools of thought would be distinguished: a 'hard' Eurasian orientation that aims essentially at recreating the Soviet Union under Russian auspices, either with the help of the CIS or through a series of bilateral treaties; a moderate Eurasian orientation that proceeds from the assumption that the vital interests of

Russia lie in that area and that effective foreign and security policies can only be conducted after stabilisation of the post-communist geopolitical space; and a Euro-Atlantic orientation that aims at broad cooperation with Western Europe, the United States and Japan (Japan in this sense being 'Western' rather than 'Asian').[15] After an unambiguously pro-Western and Euro-Atlantic orientation associated with Foreign Minister Kozyrev in the first year of Russia's existence as an independent state, it is at present the moderate Eurasian line that has become dominant.

Russia as a partner in European security

One of the most authoritative expressions of this line can be found in the *Basic Principles of Foreign Policy of the Russian Federation*, a document whose importance lies in the fact that it was agreed upon by all the major institutions involved in foreign policy-making, including the Foreign Ministry, the Ministry for Foreign Economic Relations, the Defence Ministry, the intelligence services, the Defence Council and two parliamentary committees (on foreign affairs and foreign economic relations, and on defence and security). Yuri Skokov, the then secretary of the Defence Council, had overall responsibility for drafting the document.[16]

Russia's vital interests are clearly enumerated there. In addition to the 'integrity of the Russian Federation', the developments that would threaten Russia's vital interests are held to be the 'disruption of integration processes in the CIS, violation of human rights and freedoms, military conflicts in neighbouring countries' and 'steps that are aimed at the weakening and disruption of the international position of Russia'.[17]

In external affairs, the relationship with the countries of the former Soviet Union is regarded as being of crucial importance. It is noteworthy, therefore, that Russia itself could not develop normally if the house built on the post-Soviet geopolitical space were not put in order. The architectural design evident in the document therefore includes principles such as the 'creation of an effective system of collective defence', ensuring the status of Russia as the single nuclear power in the CIS, strengthening the external borders of the Commonwealth and maintaining its military infrastructure and installations. There should also be a 'peacemaking mechanism in the framework of new integration and with the participation of Russia, including on the basis of a mandate by the UN or the CSCE [Conference on Security and Cooperation in Europe]'.

There are two noteworthy features that distinguish this document from the *Foreign Policy Concept of the Russian Federation* which was completed by the Russian Foreign Ministry in October of the previous year.[18] First, the Defence Council document displays a greater sense of self-confidence. This is evident, for instance, in the claim that Russia, 'despite the crisis which it is experiencing, remains one of the great powers due to its potential as well as its influence on the course of world events'. Second, the document reverses the priorities between the United States and Europe. It focuses less on the former and more on the latter, and supports close cooperation with both Western and Central and Eastern Europe.

Close reading of the *Basic Principles* warrants the conclusion that, at least at the conceptual level, Western security interests and vital Russian interests for the most part coincide. This concerns first and foremost the objective of preventing the huge landmass of Eurasia from becoming a breeding ground for instability. It is noteworthy, therefore, that Russian foreign-policy practice has not been far removed from the concepts. Looking at both theory and practice, the following propositions concerning Russian–European congruence and commonalities of interest can be made.

– *Regional political and economic integration*. The re-establishment of integrative processes and mechanisms serves both Western and Russian interests. This applies also to the difficult relationship between Russia and Ukraine. The mid-July 1993 agreement between Russia, Ukraine and Belarus to form a Common Market for goods, services and capital is therefore to be applauded.[19] A greater Western role in managing and moderating the Ukrainian–Russian conflict, however, is still called for.

– *Regional security cooperation*. The fact that Russia has not looked favourably upon attempts, initiated primarily by Ukraine, to construct a buffer zone or union of states between the Baltic and the Black Sea (BBSU) should not cause too much concern. Popular-front organisations from Ukraine, Belarus, Lithuania, Moldova and Poland met in Minsk in June 1993. Several of the governments of those states slated to form a new *cordon sanitaire* have fortunately been lukewarm towards the idea, fearing that they may be drawn into taking Ukraine's side in its conflicts with Russia over nuclear weapons, the Black Sea Fleet and the status of the Krim.

– *Border control*. Russia and the West need more border control. This would keep in check international criminal gangs, smuggling, drug trafficking, the illicit trade in radioactive materials and the proliferation of conventional and nuclear weapons. It is primarily, if not exclusively, Russia that has the resources to cope with such problems.

– *Migration and refugees*. Violent conflicts on CIS territory ultimately affect Western security and other interests because wars create refu-

gees. The number of 'internal' CIS refugees in Russia today is officially about 800,000, the true figure probably being much higher.
Refugees are a drain on Russian resources and diminish the chances of
successful economic reform – and they could 'spill over'. Although the
threat of several million Russian and other CIS refugees streaming first
into Eastern and Central and then into Western Europe is probably
exaggerated, perfect control of would-be migrants is impossible. Even
imperfect control is impossible without Russian cooperation and ultimately without greater economic stability.

– *Peacekeeping and peacemaking*. The United Nations (UN), the
CSCE, the North Atlantic Treaty Organisation (NATO) and other
international institutions are by their very nature and function unable
effectively to address internal CIS conflicts. Typical examples include
the war between Armenia and Azerbaijan over Nagorno-Karabakh, the
fighting between Abkhazia and Georgia, ethnic strife in the North
Caucasus and border transgressions from Afghanistan into Tajikistan.
One of the main lessons from the nightmare in Bosnia-Herzegovina
may very well be that at times only peacemaking – that is, the use of
force – can prevent protracted killing and rape. But given recent
precedents it is difficult to conceive of any European country other
than Russia willing to commit forces for such purposes on CIS territory.

– *Islamic fundamentalism and Western values*. Islamic fundamentalism or radicalism is one of the main threats to Western, not just
American, interests worldwide. Competition for the domestic- and
foreign-policy orientation of the Muslims in the Caucasus and Central
Asia has only just begun. And to the extent that Russia incorporates
Western values, its efforts should be supported. It is ineffective to
leave the task of competing simply to Turkey.

Turning to the more specific issues of conventional and nuclear
weapons in European security, the following propositions are worth
examining.

– *Prevention of nuclear proliferation*. Russia has played an admirable
and largely successful role in preventing the proliferation of the former
Soviet Union's huge arsenal of nuclear weapons. After the disintegration of the USSR, Russia declared itself primarily responsible for a
total of approximately 27,000 nuclear warheads. By July 1992 the
transfer of all tactical nuclear weapons to Russia had been completed.
There have been many reports of the unauthorised transfer of nuclear
weapons to countries in the Middle East, but none of these reports have
been substantiated. A similar success story can be told about the
thousands of Russian nuclear scientists and missile engineers: despite
the fact that they would be welcome and well paid in several countries

to help build up a nuclear potential, they have stayed put in their own country or gone to work for research institutions in the West.

– *Curbing nuclear arms competition and testing.* Russia has sensibly opposed the resumption of nuclear testing, thereby discouraging other nuclear powers from breaking the moratorium. In the Strategic Arms Reduction Talks (START) I Treaty it agreed to deep cuts in its long-range nuclear arsenal, and in START II abandoned the principle of parity and consented to further severe cuts. Moscow is continuing to demand the transfer of ex-Soviet strategic weapons to Russia and, through the ratification of START I by Kazakhstan and Belarus, has come closer to that goal. Only Ukraine is holding out.

– *No nuclear weapons for Ukraine.* Concerning the temptation in Ukraine to renege on its commitment to ratify START I and accede to the Nuclear Non-Proliferation Treaty (NPT), Western and Russian security interests also coincide. The idea of Ukraine as a nuclear power should be abhorrent not only because of the dangers of nuclear proliferation, but for other reasons as well. As the Ukrainian Foreign Minister, Anatoly Zlenko, told parliament in the June 1993 debate on the possible ratification of START I, the state did not have facilities for enriching uranium and plutonium; lacked safe means for protecting the environment from nuclear contamination; did not have and could not provide a nuclear testing ground; and would need up to $100bn to acquire and maintain a viable nuclear force.[20] Considering the dismal state of the economy, a *force de frappe* is the last thing the country needs.

– *Conventional arms reductions.* Russia is living up to both its commitments under the Conventional Armed Forces in Europe (CFE) Treaty and the subsequent Vienna accord on maximum numbers of ground and air forces, thereby contributing to a reduction in the level of conventional arms and armed forces in Europe.

Russia, to summarise, has looked at Europe from institutionalist and idealist perspectives rather than through realist or neo-realist lenses. Exemplary for the new, primarily civilian and civil conceptual approach is the relationship with Germany. There are a number of developments which would cause concern if the government in Moscow were to interpret them from traditionalist perspectives: the restiveness of ethnic Germans on Russian soil; the special interest of Germany in the Kaliningrad oblast; the *Sachwalter* and *Vermittler* role the German Foreign Office has openly asserted in the controversies between Russia and the Baltic states over Russian troop presence and minorities there; the expansion of German economic and political influence in Poland, the Czech Republic, Slovakia and Hungary; and the likely

extension of this influence to Ukraine. None of these familiar ghosts of
the past seem to matter very much.

Yet this picture is (almost) too good to be true. It is still right to
compare Russian policies to an orchestra playing a theme that is
pleasing to the Euro-Atlantic ear. But at the same time, in the background, are audible, quite different and less harmonious themes that,
although played *piano*, could become dominant – particularly if some
of the flutes and violins were to be replaced by brass sections from the
conservative opposition forces, including the military, that helped
defeat the more radical and fundamentalist opposition in October
1993.

Russia as a risk factor in European security
Russia's at present primarily cooperative stance in European security
affairs could change to more threatening attitudes and policies if three
conditions were to be fulfilled. Such conditions would be met if:
Russia were to experience a significant failure in any one of the main
transformation processes mentioned above; a coalition of former com-
munists, nationalists and fascists were to succeed in overthrowing the
government; Yeltsin himself were to preside over a shift or drift from a
'moderate' to a 'hard' assertion of Russian interests in the post-Soviet
geopolitical space.

Evidently, the danger of a 'red–brown' coalition taking over (danger number two) could arise if the socio-economic order were on the
brink of collapse or the Federation on the verge of disintegration. As
this paper has attempted to show, although it is impossible to rule out
anything in Russia, there are at present several encouraging trends
towards stabilisation. Hence, the risk of a coup or collapse is less
pronounced than the danger of Russian policy drifting in a 'hard'
direction (danger number three).

There are several features of current policies that already embody a
'hard' neo-imperialist approach and conform to the idea of an unpleasant background theme that could become dominant. Take, for instance,
the idea of 'special rights' for Russia in the CIS. In February 1993,
Yeltsin said that Russia 'continues to have a vital interest in the
cessation of all armed conflicts on the territory of the former USSR'.
However, he went on to say that:

> The world community is increasingly coming to understand Rus-
> sia's special responsibility in this difficult task. I think the moment
> has come when responsible international organisations, including
> the United Nations, should grant Russia special powers as a guaran-
> tor of peace and stability in the region of the former Union. Russia

has a heartfelt interest in stopping all armed conflicts on the territory of the former Soviet Union.[21]

Russian representatives at the UN and the North Atlantic Cooperation Council (NACC) were later at pains to deny that Russia was intent on pursuing neo-imperialist policies and in effect proclaiming the equivalent of a Monroe Doctrine for Eurasia. But the problem from a Western security vantage point is that Russia cannot be regarded as a neutral party. Its peacekeeping operations and the presence of its armed forces in the CIS, the Baltic and Georgia (without any stationing of forces agreements) serve more or less well-conceived Russian interests; these, as outlined in the previous section, often match Western interests, but at times do not. One of the examples of such ambiguity is the Russian 'peacekeeping' operation in Moldova. Russian forces of the 14th Army stationed there openly supported the Russian minority in the Trans-Dniestr region; the commander of these forces, General Aleksandr Lebed, bluntly asserted that they would not leave until the political status of the Trans-Dniestr region was clearly defined.[22] In the meantime, Russians are consolidating their control of what in essence has become an independent mini-Soviet republic, and taking revenge against those who opposed its establishment. The Trans-Dniestr courts even charge these opponents with 'acts of terrorism against the Soviet state' in violation of Article 6 of the criminal code of a non-existing legal entity: the Soviet Union.

The Trans-Dniestr affair is noteworthy for another feature. It marked the first time that the instruments of Tsarist expansionism, the Cossacks, took a hand in supporting the Russian-speaking population. Rather than putting them in their place, Yeltsin has put them on the political map. He has signed decrees in 'support of the Cossack revival movement and the restoration of Cossack economic, cultural and patriotic traditions and forms of self-government' and allowed them to create their own military units within the Russian Army.[23] Cossacks have duly made a nuisance of themselves in other Eurasian hot spots, notably in the Northern Caucasus and the Transcaucasus, and made their (Russian) loyalties clear in the controversies with Ukraine.

Another example of policies on or over the brink of neo-imperialist approaches is Russia's stance in the Baltic region. There are two opposing sets of perceptions and interests here: that of the Baltic nations, which did not invite the Russian presence, military or civilian, but which have in principle reconciled themselves to the idea that the Russian minority ought to be given residency and citizenship rights provided they meet certain minimum conditions; and that of the Russians, who would like to retain the rights and privileges they enjoyed in the Soviet period. The nationalist right in Russia has turned this issue into a stick with which to beat the government, especially the Foreign Ministry. But on this issue Yeltsin himself has taken a hard line without necessarily reacting to nationalist pressures.

In July 1993, for instance, in talks with Chancellor Kohl of Germany in Irkutsk, he reinstated the at times officially denied link between the withdrawal of Russian forces and citizenship rights. The troops would be pulled back '*if* the problems of the Russian-speaking population will be solved in a just manner and *if* there is no discrimination in these states against the Russian population'.[24] Whereas subsequently Russian troops were withdrawn from Lithuania, they are still in Estonia and Latvia to support Russian interests.

Doubt as to the disinterested use of the 'instruments of peace' also arises when looking at the conflict between Abkhazia and Georgia. Paradoxically, but not untypically for the state of affairs in many of the 'titular' republics inside and outside Russia, the Abkhazians account for only 18% of the population in 'their' republic, but are doing well militarily against the Georgians (46% of the population in Abkhazia) and the Georgian armed forces. It is difficult to believe that their relative success could have been achieved without Russian help. The controversial question is only at what level such assistance has been provided and who – in Moscow or in the region – has authorised it.

As noted, information on these matters is difficult to verify. No such difficulty applies to the disinclination of many Russians to accept the independence of the successor states as final and to resign themselves to the loss of influence and control in the Caucasus, the Baltic area and in Central and Eastern Europe. Such aversion is apparent in particular in relation to Ukraine. Current widespread Russian opinion has it that the return of Ukraine to the Russian fold (not necessarily as a constituent part of the Russian Federation, but in close association) is simply a matter of time. This facile view is predicated on the assumption that Ukraine is in the midst of a severe economic and political crisis with its large Russian population increasingly disenchanted with its original support for Ukrainian independence; as time goes by, they will demand reintegration with Russia. The potential for dangerous consequences deriving from a disintegration of Ukraine and attendant Russian intervention for all of Central and Eastern Europe, affecting, among other countries, Poland, the Czech Republic, Slovakia and Hungary, does not need to be underlined. But the current Russian mood is well exemplified by such gestures of defiance as the overwhelming vote by the Russian parliament (166 to zero with one abstention) rejecting the intended division of the Black Sea Fleet and declaring the naval city of Sevastopol to be Russian territory.[25]

Tendencies towards a greater assertion of Russian self-interest and *samostoiatel'nost'* (self-sufficiency) are evident also when examining recent Russian arms-export policy. Nationalists have claimed that the military–industrial complex, despite all the disruptions, is the only sector of the economy capable of successfully competing with the Western industrialised countries. They have asserted that Russian support for Western sanctions against Yugoslavia, Iraq and Libya has cost Russia about $16bn in lost contracts, and point out that the sums lost by far exceed what Russia ever got or will ever get in Western economic assistance. The Foreign Ministry has denied the validity of such calculations, but the facts are that Russian arms exports have declined sharply in recent years, from a fairly stable $12bn a year in the late 1980s to $3.9bn in 1991; and that Russia has made a determined effort to regain lost positions. In the process it has exported weapons of all sorts to countries which are, from a Western perspective, a security risk.

Conclusions
The break-up of the Soviet empire – in contrast to that of many other empires in the past – has proceeded with relatively little violence. The bloodshed that has occurred has been at the Russian periphery, not in its heartland. Thus far, Russia has conducted a Western-oriented policy in the 'far abroad', and a course of moderate attempts to restore Russian influence in the 'near abroad'. The primary determinants of such policies have been the exigencies of the domestic transformation processes and the constraints imposed by economic weakness. But there is as yet no end to the debate about Russia's identity and Russian 'national interests'.

The current tendency in Russian foreign and security policies is definitely one of greater assertiveness compared to the country's first year as the main successor state to the Soviet Union. This is in part due to the internal power struggles which frequently bend foreign policy in unexpected and, from the Western viewpoint, unwelcome directions. But it is probably also the result of a measure of perceived stabilisation. It is doubtful, however, whether this tendency towards assertiveness will become more pronounced and lead to a comprehensive revision of foreign policy. Stabilisation is likely to be a slow and painful process, and the above constraints will probably continue to be operative for a long time.

According to one Western view, the transformation processes in Russia follow their own logic. There is, from that perspective, nothing or very little the West can do to exert influence. Such notions are, in the author's view, essentially incorrect and politically counterproductive. Economic and technical assistance, if organised properly, can be an important factor in sustaining and accelerating change in Russia. Politically, too, the important thing for the West is to remain engaged to the maximum extent possible and in turn to make every effort to involve Russia in the Euro-Atlantic community.

Theoretically, there are three possible forms such involvement could take: extra-institutional cooperation; full membership; and association. Cooperation outside the European institutional framework (the first option) allocates an all-too-special status to Russia and almost symbolically pushes it outside existing frameworks. This first option therefore is probably best avoided.

The second option (Russia's integration into established Western institutions), however, is not viable either. This applies above all to Russian membership of the EC and NATO, both of which require a community of values, some measure of stability and predictability of the socio-economic and political system, and acceptance of the principle of supranationality. For other institutions, such as the CSCE and the Council of Europe, full participation is a lesser problem. In general, however, given Russia's huge economic, social and nationality problems, integrative processes within Russia and the CIS probably have to precede in-depth integration with Western economic and defence organisations.

The third option (association with the central Western institutions in conjunction with full membership in others) remains the best course. Viable manifestations of this approach are continued membership and cooperation with Russia in the CSCE (where Russia is a full member) and in NACC, and the intended ersatz association of Russia with the EC in the form of a treaty on cooperation and partnership.

Constructive Western engagement in the Russian transformation process is no guarantee that Russia will remain a partner in European security, but it can lessen the danger of that country once again becoming a threat.

Notes

[1] A May 1993 report by Anders Aslund of the Stockholm Institute for East European Economic Research considers the fall of GNP in 1992 to have been only 7%; see Wall Street Journal, European edition, 25–26 June 1993; and Delovoi mir, no. 17, 21 May 1993, p. 4.

This paper has been updated to take into account Yeltsin's dissolution of parliament on 21 September 1993, the legislature's resistance and counter-offensive, and the restoration of control by the President on 4 October, all of which took place after the IISS Annual Conference. The updating did not make it necessary to revise the argument.

[2] 'How to Rescue Russia', The Economist, 3 July 1993, p. 70.

[3] Elisabeth Rubinstein, 'Economists See Signs of Russian Turnaround As Inflation, Production Show Improve-

ment', *Wall Street Journal*, European edition, 25–26 June 1993.
[4] According to Boris Fedorov, the Russian Vice-President and Finance Minister, as quoted in 'Russland will in Tokio nicht Bittsteller sein', *Frankfurter Allgemeine Zeitung*, 6 July 1993. Such estimates, however, assume that a package of financial stabilisation was put in place.
[5] Anatolii Chubais as quoted in *ibid.*; see also 'The Revolution Begins', *The Economist*, 3 July 1993, p. 69.
[6] 'Armiia – prizyv bez otveta', *Rossiiskie vesti*, 25 May 1993.
[7] *Ibid.*
[8] 'Rossiiskaia armiia. Novye vremena: Interv'iu ministra oborony RF Pavla Gracheva', *Nezavisimaia gazeta*, 8 June 1993. 'Ei-bogu, dusha raduetsia' is the Russian original of his proclaimed enthusiasm.
[9] 'Armiia – prizyv bez otveta'.
[10] Andrei Kozyrev, 'Partiia voiny nastupaet – i v Moldove, i v Gruzii, i v Rossii', *Izvestiya*, 30 June 1992.
[11] 'Vesti', evening news programme, Russian television; see also Aleksandr Zhilin, 'Army and the President: Full Understanding', *Moscow News* (Moscow), no. 25, 18 June 1993, p. 10.
[12] 'Rossiiskaia armiia'.
[13] One of the best analyses of these facts and factors is provided by Al'gis Prazauskas, 'Razval Rossii – eto politicheskii blef: Giperkinez "natsional'nogo voprosa"', *Nezavisimaia gazeta*, 28 May 1993. The author is a senior researcher at the Institute for Eastern Research (Institut vostokovedeniia) at the Russian Academy of Sciences.
[14] These and other demographic data (unless indicated otherwise) are taken from the 1989 census; see *Natsional'nyi sostav naseleniia* (Moscow: Informatsionno-izdatel'skii tsentr, 1989), and *Vestnik statistiki*, no. 10, 1990.
[15] This sensible differentiation was suggested to the author by Heinz Timmerman of the Bundesinstitut für ostwissenschaftliche und internationale Studien, Cologne.
[16] The full title of the document is *Basic Principles of a Foreign Policy Concept of the Russian Federation*. Thus far the only publicly available summary of its origins and content, together with excerpts, is by Vladislav Chernov, 'Natsional'nye interesy Rossii i ugrozy dlia ee bezopasnosti', *Nezavisimaia gazeta*, 29 April 1993. The author is Deputy-Head of the Department for Strategic Security at the Russian Security Council.
[17] 'Natsional'nye interesy Rossii'.
[18] 'Kontsepsiia vneshnei politiki Rossiiskoi Federatsii', unpublished (mimeograph); on the background of the *Foreign Policy Concept's* origins and content, see *Nezavisimaia gazeta*, 21 October 1992.
[19] ITAR-TASS and Interfax, 11 July 1993.
[20] *The Moscow Times* and *The Moscow Tribune*, 4 June 1993.
[21] In his speech to a congress of the Civic Union, a centre-right alliance, in late February 1993; ITAR-TASS, 1 March 1993.
[22] Serge Schmemann, 'Yeltsin Suggests Russian Regional Role', *New York Times*, 1 March 1993.
[23] Fred Kaplan, 'A Russian Warrior Culture Revives,' *The Boston Globe*, 2 January 1993.
[24] 'Kohl sagt Moskau Unterstützung zu', *Frankfurter Allgemeine Zeitung*, 12 July 1993.
[25] 'Vesti', 9 July 1993.

After Bipolarity: Germany and European Security

DR JOSEF JOFFE

Historically, Germany has not been a pillar of stability in Europe, but has acted either as a magnet or as a motor of expansionism. When weak, Germany attracted the ambitions of others; when strong, it sought to dominate them. Yet the experience of weakness has been more typical than its spurts of hegemonism. The Wilhelmine attempt at *weltpolitik* only lasted a quarter-century, from the early 1890s to 1918; Hitler's attempt ended in complete disaster after only a dozen. In both cases, German strength proved a resistible threat – impressive in the beginning, but hollow in the end.

Since the beginning of the modern state system, weakness has been Germany's more typical lot. The Thirty Years War, although ostensibly a religious quarrel, was in fact a great-power contest in and over Germany. After the Peace of Westphalia, Germany remained what it had been in war: a stake rather than a centre of power. 'Germany' was only a geographical and cultural expression, a motley collection of some two dozen kingdoms, principalities and cities squeezed by France in the west and the Habsburgs in the east. Even the rise of Prussia in the eighteenth century could not dispatch Germany's endemic insecurity. Frederick the Great could grab a few conquests here and there, but, by 1756, he found himself embroiled in the Seven Years War and soon encircled by an all-European coalition. That calamity was to be repeated twice – and more brutally each time – in the First and Second World Wars.

Paradoxically, Germany was fated to be a source of instability in both weakness and strength. This paradox is more easily resolved than most, and its key lies in a geography which thrust Germany into the centre of Europe. Germany was too strong to be left alone and too weak to 'go it alone'. At the fulcrum of the European balance, the country had to invite domination when weak. In strength, Germany reached for hegemony to escape from endemic vulnerability once and for all – either diplomatically, as under Bismarck, or militarily, in the case of Wilhelm II and Hitler. But whenever Germany tried to seize supremacy, it was beaten back with ever more cataclysmic results. Germany, as Ludwig Dehio put it so aptly, was never more than a 'semi-hegemonic power', with offensive capabilities always outstripping defensive ones.

By contrast, the Cold Peace of the second half of the twentieth century, from partition in 1945 to Unification II in 1990, proved an unmitigated blessing in the ebb and flow of European stability. For the first time, Germany was neither too weak nor too strong; it could neither threaten nor be threatened. Some believe that it was partition that had brought about this wondrous state of affairs, but that is to confuse the smoke with the fire or the epiphenomenon with the cause. Partition was simply another consequence of bipolarity which divided Germany and the continent between two blocs and two superpowers.

Although this outcome was low on justice, it was high on stability, with the bipolar conflict spawning and cementing a peculiar kind of order. The 'Long Peace', to use John L. Gaddis' term, had three mainstays.

First, vast concentrations of ever-ready nuclear and conventional forces reminded both antagonists of the classic precept of the bipolar age: whosoever shoots first will die second. Hence war, whether pre-emptive or preventive, was out of the question, and ultra-stability prevailed over deadly fear or murderous ambition. As a result, politics – and thus stability – became frozen wherever the balance of terror ruled (virtually across the entire northern hemisphere from Seattle to Sakhalin). No matter how contested, borders remained cast in concrete; no matter how fiery, national ambitions remained in check.

Second, bipolarity spelled control. Precisely because great-power war implied mutual extinction, the United States and the USSR made sure that unruly allies would not drag them into war. Even war between informal allies – above all, in the Middle East – was quickly contained by the two superpowers for fear of being sucked into the quarrels of minor ones.

Third, bipolarity made for stability within blocs and nations. Beholden to the security extended by patrons, clients took care not to affront or alienate their protectors. Running on a short leash of dependence, lesser allies accepted the discipline meted out by the strong. Amongst themselves, dependents remained on their best behaviour because of an overweening security threat from without. The rigorous integration of military forces repressed whatever temptations may have riled the soul. (The one exception was the war between Greece and Turkey over Cyprus in 1974.) In the Soviet sphere, deviationism was swiftly suppressed by invasion. Even internally, within states, discipline prevailed among unhappy nationalities, given the centralising pressures exerted by the Cold War.

Bipolarity was anchored in the heart of Europe, where the global, regional and intranational balance came together in Germany, a veritable microcosm of the old order. Along the Elbe River, the two superpowers, the two blocs and the two Germanys were fused together in a triple-tiered structure of ultra-stable confrontation. The US and the Soviet Union positioned the bulk of their forward-stationed forces in Germany. Between the Rhine and the Oder, the two alliances deployed 1.3 million men plus thousands of nuclear weapons. And the two successor states of the Reich, with a sum total of 600,000 troops, were caught in a peculiar kind of stalemate that simultaneously harnessed and neutralised German power.

This arrangement was truly unique in the annals of German and European history. Sheltered by two mighty blocs which could no longer countenance war, post-war Germany enjoyed a degree of security that had eluded all its predecessors in this millennium. Nor could Germany toy with the offensive strategies that had animated (and undone) the Second and Third Reich; both German states were powerfully contained and constrained by the very same system that gave them a surfeit of security. Post-war Germany, in short, had lost autonomy in matters of security which, in the past, had proven pernicious to both German security and European stability.

For Germany could never quite measure up to the task when forced to provide for its own security. Prior to Unification I (in 1871), Germany regularly ended up as venue and victim of war by dint of political disunion and geographic vulnerability. Thereafter, this Central European power-house boasted great strength, but its reach still fell short of its grasp. No matter how strong, Germany would always galvanise an even stronger anti-German coalition, and so initial victory turned twice into final defeat. By contrast, the bipolar stalemate system blessed both Germany and Europe to a greater extent than either had experienced in the past.

Already the object of nostalgic memories, that ultra-stable system is now dead and gone. Soviet power first collapsed and then retracted almost all the way to Moscow. American power is rapidly receding across the Atlantic. One alliance, the Warsaw Treaty Organisation, has vanished; the other, the North Atlantic Treaty Organisation (NATO), stays in place, but bereft of a real role and mission above and beyond that of a multilateral reinsurance treaty with a shrinking military panoply.

Predictably, the demise of the *ancien système* has not increased stability in Europe, certainly not along its south-eastern periphery. Iraq's lunge into Kuwait occurred less than three weeks after President Mikhail Gorbachev had conceded defeat in the Cold War by granting

German reunification under Western auspices (during his summit with Chancellor Kohl in Stavropol on 16 July 1990). The war in Yugoslavia broke out the following summer. Neither war would surely have erupted if Soviet power had still been intact. Moscow would not have allowed its Iraqi client to attack a neighbour firmly ensconced among America's possessions. And in Yugoslavia, the brooding presence of a mighty USSR would have continued to contain the mortal tensions built into that shaky federal construction. Now, low-level war is besetting the former Soviet Union along its southern reaches; and latent war is brewing between Ukraine and Russia.

In the first test of post-Cold War stability, the rest of Europe has proved unable to contain or cope with the war in the Balkans. Nor will the partition of Bosnia between Croatia and Serbia heal the wound. The Bosnian Muslims will continue to fight, and with the Bosnian buffer gone, the two victors will not sit still for long digesting their booty. There are too many unsettled accounts and boundaries to promise lasting peace between Croats and Serbs.

By benign contrast, Europe west of the Oder River remains a haven of peace. In that respect, Western Europe resembles Europe in the aftermath of the Napoleonic wars. There are no major conflicts; indeed, there are no conflicts with a military potential anywhere between Biscay and Bug. None of the key powers suffer from a military threat, and it is hard to foresee the emergence of such tensions on the horizon of political reality.

For the first time in history Germany finds itself in an enviable, historically unique strategic position. It has no claims against its neighbours, and they have no claims against Germany.[1] Indeed, for the first time in the annals of unified statehood, Germany is surrounded only by friends. One 'arch enemy', France, is tied to Germany in a heavily institutionalised relationship that is frequently labelled an 'axis'. Another, Russia, has become a great-power-in-waiting: economically prostrate and virtually ungovernable. Geographically, Russian power is now at the farthest remove ever. During the Cold War, the Soviet Union was literally encamped in Germany. When the last Russian troops are withdrawn in 1994, by contrast, Germany will be separated from Russia by Poland, the Baltic states, Belarus and Ukraine – by a buffer about a thousand miles wide.

To the west, Germany is part of an economic and semi-political community stretching from the Oder to the Atlantic and sheltered by American might. To the east, ancient conflicts are but a painful memory; Poland, the Czech Republic and Slovakia, indeed all the former members of the Warsaw Pact, look to Germany for aid, markets and diplomatic support in Western councils. And the war in the south-east does not pose a strategic threat to Germany. Threats that do impinge on Germany are either remote, diffuse or non-military: uncontrollable immigration from east and south-east; nuclear reactor safety in Eastern Europe; political instability in the former Soviet republics; and, farther afield, long-range weapons of mass destruction in the Middle East and the Maghreb. Since the beginning of the European state system, in short, Germany's strategic position has never been more secure. Even at the height of Bismarck's power, when Germany ruled Europe for at least 20 years, the Reich had to be *toujours en vedette* (as Bismarck put it) against the threat of war with France, Russia and Britain.

Safety does not make for an easy grand strategy, nor for a clear thrust or determinate purpose. This problem besets all the major powers in the aftermath of the great conflict known as the Cold War. But, as usual, Germany has to juggle more balls than most, which has made for a familiar German response dating back to Frederick the Great's injunction, *garder les mains libres*. The contemporary version reads 'keep all options open', which can be broken down into the following corollary which does not necessarily add up to a harmonious set of axioms:

– Maintain NATO and, above all, the US security tie as the ultimate insurance against the resurgence of a Russian threat. As in the past, the Atlantic anchor and counterweight reassures not only Germany, but also its neighbours by removing the sting of the country's power and centrality in the European balance. But at the same time, keep intact a continental option centred on

– the special relationship with France, as institutionalised in the Treaty of Friendship and Cooperation of 1963 and epitomised militarily by the Franco-German Corps. One part of this arrangement is fed by sheer sentiment, since it was the clasp of hands across the Rhine that smoothed West Germany's re-entry into the community of nations after the Second World War. The other part rests on hard-headed interest, with each of the two regarding (and manipulating) the other as an indispensable partner in the leadership of Europe. Yet, for precisely this reason, the 'axis' contains numerous rivalries which spell out the imperative: limit dependence on France and take care not to alienate other European allies by preserving

– a subsidiary British tie, especially since some German interests – like free trade or the widening of the European Community (EC) – are better served by London than by Paris. Hence, Bonn is also cultivating a relationship with Britain, as exemplified metaphorically by the term 'The Silent Alliance' and militarily by regular bilateral consultations and the air-mobile division (with Britain, Holland and Belgium) within

NATO's Rapid Reaction Corps. To complement this triple-tiered Western relationship, reunified Germany has not forsaken its
– Russian option, even though Moscow now has very little with which to blackmail or bribe Germany. In the past, West Germany's exposure to Soviet military might and the Soviet veto over inter-German relations made willy-nilly for a 'separate détente' and a good deal of propitiatory behaviour on the part of Bonn. But after reunification and the retraction of Soviet power, accompanied by tens of billions in ransom money, the 'Moscow connection' has dwindled into a latent option – not so much to be used now as to be kept for future contingencies. For the time being
– the stabilisation of Germany's immediate Central European hinterland is the more urgent task. Like Britain, Germany has been more eager than most to extend the shelter of Western institutions eastwards
– at least to Poland, the Czech Republic, Slovakia and Hungary. This strategy makes sense economically and geographically. Economically, these countries, above all the Czech Republic and Slovakia, are Germany's 'Mexico': next door, and with workforces that offer high productivity rates at about one-tenth of German wage levels. Their markets are ideally suited for penetration, but this requires stable political evolution. Hence Germany is in the forefront of those who would attach this Central European group to the EC and NATO while taking care not to do so too blatantly for fear of alienating Russia.

As should be self-evident, these options do not add up to a coherent whole bereft of contradictions; the 'French connection' does not harmonise with the Atlantic one, and the Central European option clashes with the Russian relationship. Other things remaining equal, German will pursue a strategy of diversification, balance and compensation, trying to give unto Peter without taking from Paul and to evade irrevocable commitment.

Above all, and in the absence of a resurgent strategic threat, a united Germany will try to do what it knows best: to act as a 'civilian power' and to eschew for as long as possible the ways of a traditional great power and hence the use of force.

The war in the former Yugoslavia is a case in point. No one was more adamant about the need to recognise the breakaway republics of Croatia and Slovenia than Germany. Yet no one was more insistent on staying out of the aftermath. Government and opposition proclaimed in unison that both the history and the constitution of Germany forbade intervention in the conflict. Both Chancellor Helmut Kohl and the parliamentary leader of the Social Democrats, Hans-Ulrich Klose, insisted at the Munich Wehrkunde Conference in February 1993 that German troops could not set foot on soil once trampled by the

Wehrmacht. (As was pointed out, this left only Sweden, Switzerland and Portugal as legitimate objects of pacification.) Naturally, the abstention of Europe's strongest conventional power did not enhance the eagerness of France, Britain and Italy to deploy combat troops to the Balkan theatre.

The third year after division thus belied widespread expectations about the emergence of a 'Fourth Reich'. If Germany reborn displayed ambitions for a greater role, it did so fitfully and without a coherent grand strategy. There was, to be sure, a German power-play in the run-up to the EC-wide recognition of Croatia and Slovenia in January 1992, with Bonn wielding the implied threat of unilateral recognition to pressure the other 11 members of the EC. But that was the end of the game. Germany did not forge ahead to act – Bismarck-like – as the prime mediator in the Balkan conflict. Even less did Bonn take the lead in harnessing a military coalition against Serbia.

Another thrust aimed at a permanent seat on the United Nations (UN) Security Council, but again rather fitfully and timidly. Unlike Japan, which is lobbying hard for these laurels, Germany has chosen discretion over ambition. Bonn remains well aware of the obstacles. For one, there is France which, in spite of the vaunted Franco-German 'axis', does not look benevolently at a future in which it might have to share its exalted UN status with Germany. Second, Germany is only too conscious of its handicaps. To take its seat among the certified great powers, Germany would have to act like one – that is, to use force for purposes other than self- or alliance defence. Yet that capability remains seriously constrained. One hurdle is judicial, all three major parties (CDU/CSU, SPD, FDP) having thrown the issue of force projection into the lap of the Constitutional Court in 1993. The second hurdle is political. Even if the Court issues a permissive ruling, there remains a deeply ingrained aversion to the use of force in society at large.

Three factors have shaped German abstentionism: the Constitution; the legacy of the Second World War; and the habits acquired in 40 years of non-autonomy in matters of security.

The Constitution

The prevailing interpretation, at least until 1992, stated that German troops were allowed into action only in case of a direct attack on Germany or NATO. The Article of the Basic Law quoted most often in support of that position is 87a, which states: 'Except for defence, the armed forces may be used only for purposes expressly authorised by this Basic Law'.[2] Yet a closer look at this article, as well as a perusal of the standard commentaries, reveals that the injunction 'defence only' limits the use of the military in domestic settings – when a state of emergency rules, for instance, or in cases of natural disaster. Like so much of German constitutional law, Article 87 is rooted in the Weimar experience when the army was used and misused in domestic power plays.

Article 24, on the other hand, stakes out a wide area of permissiveness. It explicitly authorises the federal government to take part in systems of 'mutual collective security' and thus opened the way for (West) Germany's membership of NATO and the Western European Union (WEU). 'Collective security' is also at the heart of the UN Charter which, under Article 43, enjoins member-states to contribute military forces to the Security Council for peacekeeping and peace-enforcement (i.e., combat) purposes. When the Federal Republic acceded to the UN in 1973, it accepted all obligations under the Charter. Whence it follows that Bonn implicitly conceded its legal ability to honour these obligations.

Why, then, the insistence, crystallising in the 1980s and originally shared by all political parties, on stringent constitutional limits? The heart of the matter is not juridical, but historical and political.

History
It should not come as a surprise that a nation which twice this century failed so disastrously in war and thereafter succeeded so brilliantly in peace should remain so thoroughly attached to the habits of a 'civilian power'. To begin with, a pacifist posture served – and continues to serve – as positive proof of moral rehabilitation in the aftermath of Nazi crimes. Germans are inordinately fond of telling themselves and the world: 'We have learned our lesson'. This message breaks down into two implicit parts. One is to claim redemption in the face of an unspeakable past by contrasting the goodness of the contemporaries with the sins of the forefathers. The second part goes beyond the squaring of the moral account. By insisting that they have transcended force, Germans can go one better, conquering the moral high ground against those who once vanquished and 're-educated' them and who until this day remain wedded to the retrograde ways of war – all the way to the Falklands and the Gulf.

The profits of dependence
Moreover, this moral (or moralising) posture proved to be immensely profitable. While the US, Britain and France squandered blood and treasure on post-colonial or imperial ventures around the world, the West Germans were free to tend their own garden and to unleash an enduring 'economic miracle'. During the Cold War, Britain spent an

average of 5% of its gross national product (GNP) on defence, and the US anywhere between 5% and 10%. Yet the Federal Republic has never allocated more than 3%.

The societal gains of abstentionism may have been even more impressive. The Fourth Republic in France fell in the upheavals triggered by the war in Algeria, and the tremors of that war continued to shake de Gaulle's Fifth Republic. A similar case is that of the United States, where the war in Vietnam unleashed a domestic revolt which shook the very foundation of the republic – not to mention the 'Vietnam Syndrome' that was to beset the US into the 1990s. Compared to this kind of turmoil, the divisive debates in the Federal Republic (over rearmament in the 1950s and Euromissiles in the 1980s) look like an exercise in orderly democratic procedure.

Diplomatically, the politics of passivity turned a handsome profit, too. Whereas the US, Britain and France took on a shifting array of enemies (the Arab world, China, proxies of the Soviet Union, Iran, Iraq, diverse African potentates), the Federal Republic tried to offend none and to be friends with all: with Iraq and Iran, Israel and the Arabs, and – during the second part of the Cold War (1979–87) – with the United States and the Soviet Union. Conciliation rather than confrontation and trade rather than war was the credo of West German diplomacy during the bipolar era – all the way to the 1991 Gulf War when Bonn reflexively tried to avoid an early commitment to the American-led coalition.

The constitutional limits on the use of force claimed by the entire German political establishment (until 1992) must be seen in this three-part context. It can be reduced to a simple moral: bitter were the fruits of war, sweet those of peace. Hence, it was not a *diktat* of the Basic Law which delivered the constitutional prohibition against the use of force, but a calculated political interpretation enshrined by both the Helmut Schmidt (SPD–FDP) and the Helmut Kohl (CDU/CSU–FDP) coalitions in 1982 (just before and after the ousting of the Schmidt government in the autumn). To construe a constitutional *verboten* was an elegant way of blunting American pressure for help in the Gulf War without offending Washington. And it was also a way of submitting to the obvious: that there was absolutely no consensus on force projection at home.

The habits cemented by the profits of passivity die hard. Thus, the problem of redefining the rules of engagement ended up in the hands of the Constitutional Court in 1993, and the issue was still pending in that autumn. Having twice rejected an appeal for a temporary injunction against the deployment of Federal forces (in NATO's airborne warning and control system aircraft over the Balkans and the UN mission in

Somalia), the Court will presumably rule in favour of Helmut Kohl's Christian Democrats when it comes to a verdict on substance: what kind of action is, or is not, allowed under the Basic Law? But the issue is not truly a juridical one, but one of purpose abroad and consensus at home. Neither question will prompt a clear, let alone activist, answer even if the Court rules permissively. In Bosnia, the theatre of conflict closest to home, intervention draws a categorical 'no', uttered by all parties large and small. Since the summer of 1993, a 1,200-man Bundeswehr contingent has been stationed under the UN flag in Somalia, but – and that was the condition – at the farthest possible remove from military action. Therefore, the depth of the German commitment remains to be tested under fire.

The contemporary German paradox is this: bipolarity, hence the obsessive fear of entrapment in great-power conflict, has yielded to the expansion of strategic freedom and the reduction of the potential costs of military engagement. Russia need no longer be propitiated, and to take on Somalia is easy when that country is no longer a bipolar stake. Germany is thus freer to act than ever since 1945. On the other hand, this new freedom also breeds the freedom not to engage. When real threats are few and far between, grand strategy obeys the quip: 'If you don't know where you are going, any – or no – road will take you there'.

In the present-day German case – as was true for the Germany of Frederick, Bismarck and Weimar – all roads will be taken simultaneously, although only up to a point. If a country is surrounded only by friends, it will seek to keep them. It will want to retain a paid-up insurance policy underwritten by the United States. It will try to protect its special relationship with France, even though barely contained tensions over free trade, the role of the US, monetary policy, the evolution of the EC ('deepening' versus 'widening') and, most generally, the end of dependence on France, will make that marriage an ever rockier one. Also, while courting France, Bonn will not forsake Britain. Germany will seek to include East–Central Europe in the EC and NATO orbit and, failing that, into its own. But it will pursue a 'Greater Central-European Co-Prosperity Sphere' with prudence, taking care not to alienate Russia or to stimulate the suspicion of its Western allies.

In the pre-Cold War past, as this paper has argued, Germany was not a factor of stability in Europe. It is tempting to conclude that the progressive demise of the bipolar conflict-as-order and the dispatch of ancient fetters will turn the nation at the centre, the biggest chunk of demographic and economic power in Europe, into a factor of uncertainty once more.

But those fond of travelling the historicist road should not ignore some obvious transformations in the nature of European international politics. Setting aside the violent return of history in the east and south-east, which might yet overturn all benign assumptions, today's questions and answers are merely faint copies of the real thing in the eighteenth and nineteenth centuries. What does 'expansion' mean today? It certainly does not obey the quest for territory, one critical measure of power in centuries past. Indeed, for an advanced industrial power, 'more land' spells more agricultural surpluses and higher support payments. In the days of complementary trade, territorial control also spelled profit, and thus commerce pushed the flag. But in the post-industrial world, nations trade competitively: German Volkswagens against French Peugeots or Italian Fiats, not machine tools for cereals and coal. (There is, however, an obvious exception to the rule, pertaining to First World trade with countries awash with the strategic resource, oil.)

Capital exports used to be starring villains in Leninist interpretations of history, but today investment abroad depends, in addition to wage differentials, above all on a stable socio-political setting and not on client governments in Warsaw, Prague or Hungary. As for the use of force for power and precedence, the historian is tempted to cite an iron law from the past: all nations which became rich eventually ploughed their resources into military might and geopolitical ambition – France in the seventeenth century, Britain in the eighteenth and nineteenth centuries, Prussia-Germany after 1871, the United States and Japan at the turn of the twentieth century and China today. While this iron law may yet prove to outlast the past, it is difficult to see how it would inform the strategic behaviour of Germany and other Europeans today. For in the absence of a dominant threat, all Western Europeans are in mad pursuit of the 'peace dividend'. In the special case of Germany, this classic democratic reflex is doubly galvanised by the gargantuan bill for the rehabilitation of Eastern Germany.

There are two possible morals to this story. One breeds optimism: the paradigm change foreseen by the *philosophes* of the Enlightenment and by Kant, Spencer and Schumpeter is now truly here. Accordingly, democratic and commercial republics will hearken to the call of peace and profit, not the clamour of war and aggrandisement.[3] The other possible moral bids more scepticism. 'Once the sense of threat . . . fades or dies,' Stanley Hoffmann has observed, 'there is at last in a large part of the world [i.e., the West] an approximation of those conditions of relative harmony and renunciation of force which the liberal and social democratic ideologies of the past have considered to be our promised land'.[4] The crucial qualifier here is the disappearance of a 'sense of threat'. Hence it is by no means clear whether the 'anti-historical' conduct of Western European democracies reflects a change of paradigms or merely of parameters.

The civilianising societies of Western Europe could dispense with their violent ways because, courtesy of nuclear deterrence and a quasi-imperial protectorate in the US, war had been extruded from the system. For the time being, war remains so banished because, on the outside, the collapse of Soviet power has removed any strategic threat while, on the inside, significant remnants of the American-sponsored security community are still in place. But 1993 is only the third year after the Soviet surrender in the Cold War, and it is not pre-ordained that the old parameters which have encased the 'Long Peace' (NATO, the US presence) will endure indefinitely.

Hence the indeterminacy common to all transitions, and the contemporary one is certainly more profound than any since 1945. The questions only time will resolve, then, are these: will the European peace (outside the Balkans) stand on its own? Or was it merely the epiphenomenon of a vanishing bipolar order? If it is 'yes' to the first query, then the recourse to history will hardly enlighten us. But if peace were merely a matter of parameters rather than of a new paradigm, post-Cold War Europe should be expected to resemble Europe after 1815: exhausted from a great conflict, not yet caught up in new ones, and determined to play the game of nations by institutional rules embodied in the 'Concert of Europe'. As today, there were innumerable conferences and committees dedicated to adjudicating and containing clashes of interests. Yet, by 1822, there were already distinct divisions between liberal powers like Britain and the conservatives like Prussia, Russia and Austria, foreshadowing the great conflicts that were to torment Europe in the second half of the nineteenth century.

Today, only one thing is clear. The nations of Europe, and Germany above all, have been liberated from many shackles of the *ancien système*. This spells autonomy and the freedom to experiment with new and not-so-new combinations. The collapse of the European Monetary System between September 1992 and August 1993 (which has thrust the more perfect union envisaged at Maastricht into limbo) indicates that autonomy will be grabbed when the national interest so dictates. The Bonn government financed reunification by deferring not to the needs of Europe, but to the perceived imperatives of domestic power. This outcome should sharpen the scepticism of those who believe that Western European institutions are more than the sum of their parts.

For the time being, no hegemonial ambition or strategic conflict has emerged in Europe and, like France after 1815, yesterday's Russian claimant is being resocialised into the community of European nations. In benign contrast to 1919, the United States is determined to stay in Europe, and a mainstay of the old security order – NATO – is not cracking, but merely shedding girth. The Cold War has bequeathed an enormous tradition of cooperation to Western Europe, complete with a vast network of institutions and interdependencies which is being extended to the East. On this stage, German grand strategy will maximise options and minimise hard-and-fast commitments, seeking influence and status through multilateral institutions like the EC and the United Nations, and unilaterally only where prudence permits. But when everything is tallied, one truth can hardly be gainsaid: autonomy is growing, and the old parameters are turning into variables because the bipolar system that gave rise to them has disappeared. In such an indeterminate setting, 'tis a fool who would predict more than the obvious.

Notes

[1] One exception needs to be mentioned. Former Sudeten Germans or the descendants of those who were expelled from Czechoslovakia after the Second World War claim compensation for property lost and the right to return on an individual basis.

[2] 'Außer zur Verteidigung dürfen die Streitkräfte nur eingesetzt werden, soweit dieses Grundgesetz es ausdrücklich zuläßt'.

[3] Joseph Schumpeter opined categorically: 'Militarism . . . is rooted in the autocratic state, [and] the bourgeois is unwarlike'. 'The Sociology of Imperialisms', *Social Classes – Imperialism: Two Essays* (Cleveland, OH: The World Publishing Company, Meridian Books, 1955), p. 96.

[4] Stanley Hoffmann, *The Acceptability of Military Force*, Adelphi Paper 102 (London: Brassey's for the IISS, 1973), p. 5.

Nordic and Baltic Security in the 1990s

DR KRISTER WAHLBÄCK

In today's Europe, everyone maintains that his own country has acquired entirely new parameters for its security policy since the upheavals of 1989–91. The pertinent question is: in which respect is change in one's own region really fundamentally different from change in the rest of Europe?

With regard to the three large Nordic states – Finland, Norway and Sweden – there are two such differences.

First, while continental Western Europeans have seen Moscow's armoured divisions move back from the Fulda Gap all the way to Minsk, if not Smolensk, Nordic Western Europeans still find Russian forces where they have always been: right on the eastern border of Norway and Finland, from Murmansk on the Barents Sea to St Petersburg on the Baltic Sea.

Second, continental Western Europeans may see with some confidence how their immediate neighbours to the East – the Poles, the Czechs and the Hungarians – are finally enjoying real independence for the sovereign states which they had even under communism. Nordic Western Europeans have to be more concerned about their Estonian, Latvian and Lithuanian neighbours.

It is true that the Baltic nations gained their full independence in 1918–19 at the same time as the Polish, Czech and Hungarian nations. They were all members of the League of Nations on equal terms in 1921–39, and they were all occupied by Germans and Russians in the course of the Second World War. But the Baltic states were not restored in 1945; they were turned into Soviet republics, colonised by Russian immigrants and garrisoned by Soviet armed forces.

Thus, today they have to overcome worse handicaps than the Polish, Czech and Hungarian nations, which retained the protective shell of sovereign institutions even under Stalin and Brezhnev. The Baltic states have to establish the instruments of sovereign states from scratch, and it will take them much longer to remove the remnants of Soviet rule; indeed some of these remnants cannot and should not be removed. It will also take much longer for the Russians to accept their loss of control over the Baltic nations.

These two differences in security parameters between Nordic and continental Western Europe – the distance to Russia's armed forces, and the strength of new neighbouring states – have many implications. The most important is that uncertainties surrounding the future of Russia are even more crucial to the Nordic states than to the continentals. This, in turn, affects Nordic views on their defence needs, on the implications of European Community (EC) membership, on the North Atlantic Treaty Organisation (NATO), and on appropriate ways to assist reform in Russia and to support the consolidation of Baltic independence.

The future of Russia
The basic assumption with regard to the Russian Federation is that the transformation of Russia into a stable democracy and a growing market economy will in the end be successful. When this comes about, the proximity of the Nordic states to the new Russia will be an asset.

Traditionally, the north-western part of Russia has been of great importance for the development of this immense nation. It was here, on what was then still Swedish territory, in 1703 that Peter the Great founded the city of St Petersburg and to which he moved the seat of his government in 1712. This was to be the symbol of the opening up of Russia to the West which Peter sought in order to bring his country into the modern world.

Now St Petersburg, with its six million inhabitants and large numbers of highly skilled people, is again assuming its traditional role. North-western Russia has the potential to take the lead in the country's transformation, as it did from 1890 to 1914, when Tsarist Russia was rapidly taking off in economic terms, much to the profit of businesses in neighbouring countries.

Swedes remember that the Ericsson telephone company planned to move their headquarters from Gothenburg to St Petersburg in order to get right into the heart of their most rapidly expanding market. Similarly, the Nobel family reached out from their first base in St Petersburg to command and expand oil exploitation in the Baku region, controlling in 1913 one-quarter of the world market and competing with the Rothschilds and the Rockefellers for dominance.

Norwegians recall the old trade routes to Arkhangelsk along the coast of Norway. Today, they have their eyes fixed on the prospects for joint endeavours with Russia to exploit the immense oil and gas riches of the Barents Sea, once they have agreed on how to divide the continental shelf.

The Finns are well aware of the time a century ago when Finland, as an autonomous but impoverished Grand Duchy within the Russian

Empire, began to develop, largely thanks to its proximity to St Petersburg. Now it is Finland's modern industry which is ready to move into the promising markets east of the border, rich in resources squandered under communism.

Today, geographic distance is no longer the obstacle it once was. The Nordic states have not been cut off from direct contact with the new Russia as continental Western Europe has. This will be an asset, once Russia takes off.

It is assumed that an economically successful Russia, with its own brand of democratic system, would overcome its imperialist and messianic traditions. Inevitable conflicts and tensions with neighbours would be handled by Russia in the civilised manner of other major powers in Europe today. Thus Russia would continue to play its constructive role of recent years in the new security order, in accordance with the principles laid down in the Paris Charter of 1990, and with a weight commensurate to the great resources of the Russian nation.

On the road towards this goal, however, there will be an extended period in which proximity to Russia will raise a great many problems. Some new security risks are already beginning to pose a serious threat: nuclear power stations close to the Nordic countries which do not seem much safer than Chernobyl; illegal immigration by boat people across the Baltic Sea; and smuggling of drugs and weapons as part of the efforts of Russian crime syndicates to penetrate the Nordic countries. Perhaps at some stage, if chaos were to spread among the Russian military, these countries would have to face extortion threats by local warlords, maybe claiming to possess nuclear devices. In any case, this region will have to face a whole range of repercussions arising from the fact that the Russian–Finnish border – seen as the frontier between Russian penury and Western welfare – is the most razor-sharp frontier in today's Europe.

In retrospect, however, if things go as assumed, these will turn out to be no more than transitory problems, inevitably accompanying the collapse of the most gigantic political experiment in modern history.

There are of course other, more sinister scenarios for Russia. No one wants to indulge in speculation that might serve to weaken the present Russian leadership and turn into self-fulfilling prophecies. But neither is there any point in neglecting predictions widely discussed in Russia itself. These scenarios assume a continuing inexorable slide into social chaos and political disintegration. Some observers do not even exclude a break-up of the Russian Federation, maybe entailing the emergence of some sort of new Russian neighbour in the north of Europe, possibly with St Petersburg as the capital of a 'North-western

Russia'. But long before things get out of hand to this extent, there would surely be a shift of regime in an authoritarian and nationalist direction. Such a regime would probably come to power in a mood of frustration with the West and anger at the sinister forces plotting against Russia.

It is hard to see how any sustainable economic development could come about on the basis of internal centralisation and external seclusion. Yet, even under a temporary experiment in a doomed direction, a chauvinistic Russia may be a sufficiently unpleasant neighbour in the North of Europe – primarily for the Baltic states, but not only them. This might particularly be the case if the region is not firmly anchored in a wider Euro-Atlantic security order.

However, as indicated above, it seems more probable that Russia is moving in a direction quite favourable to its small neighbours. In a loose, decentralised federation, no leaders in Moscow would be able to extract large resources for maintaining formidable offensive military capabilities, even less to move the whole Federation into aggressive action. In short, the Russian Federation would be almost as incapable of offensive enterprises as NATO has always been. This would remain true even if Russia succeeds in attaining relative prosperity, assuming that the basic outlook of the Russian nation, beneath the surface of temporary attitudes, will be more akin to that of the Germans under the Federal Republic than of the Germans under the Weimar Republic.

But even Nordic governments subscribing to fairly optimistic assessments of Russia's future cannot discard less favourable scenarios. To return to the different security parameters of continental and Nordic Western Europeans: there is a greater tension in Nordic countries between the optimistic working hypotheses and the dismal alternatives that these countries also have to keep in mind. If things go well, the region believes that it is better placed than the continentals to make the most of commercial and other exchanges with the new Russia. If they go badly, it fears that it would be more exposed than the continentals. This explains a number of characteristics in the security policy postures of the Nordic countries.

National defence
The first characteristic concerns defence budgets. In Finland, Norway and Sweden there have not been any significant defence cuts in recent years. Of course, the Finns have not been able to maintain their record of annual defence budget increases in real terms of 3–4% since the late 1970s, but they have maintained the levels achieved in 1990. Thus, in 1992, they were able to order some 60 F-18 *Hornet* fighter aircraft, securing a truly significant upgrading of the Finnish air force in the

course of the 1990s. Further, they have provided for the modernisation of their ground forces by buying large quantities of high-quality equipment from the former East Germany at very low costs. In 1993 the Norwegians took a long-term defence decision for the 1994–98 period which implies modest reductions in funding, but radical slimming of structures. The Swedish defence decision in 1992 had the same general orientation and entailed some increase in the budget in real terms. All major political parties support the JAS 39 *Gripen* project, thus ensuring that the future Swedish air force, beginning in 1995, will be operating about 140 advanced combat aircraft second to none in cost-effectiveness and technical advancement. A second batch of 100 aircraft to be produced after the year 2000 will be necessary to provide the air force with 16 squadrons as agreed by all major political parties.

Denmark is in a slightly different situation. The Danes are the great winners among the Nordic states in terms of security gains derived from the 1989–91 revolution. They used to face Warsaw Pact naval and air bases along the Baltic coast, some 50 miles from Zealand and Copenhagen. Now the Bundesmarine controls the eastern approaches to the Danish isles, and the Russians have moved back, in relative terms, as far away from Denmark as from Belgium or the Netherlands. It is thus no wonder that the Danish armed forces have to make do with short-term defence decisions and a slow decline in appropriations.

This is not to say that the Swedish military feels confident about future appropriations. The decline in Russian conventional military capabilities cannot but raise hard questions about the tasks and size of Sweden's defence forces. Will not the restoration of an effective Russian offensive capacity require so much effort as to provide Sweden with sufficient time to build up its defences, even if it makes quite radical cuts now? It may be that Swedish defence planners will be increasingly asked to prepare for participation in international peace-keeping or peace-enforcing operations on a much larger scale than before. The task for the planners – admittedly a very difficult one – will be to find force structures and weapons platforms that could be used both in this new role and to deter possible 'existential' threats should they re-emerge.

As the logic of geography indicates, the Finnish military faces less domestic pressure in this direction, while the Danish armed forces are at present planning to devote the largest share of their resources among the Nordics to peacekeeping tasks.

The European Community
EC membership is a top priority for Finland, Norway and Sweden. The Copenhagen European Council in June settled on 1 January 1995 as

the target date for their accession. Security issues have not yet attracted much controversy as preparations are under way for the referenda campaigns in 1994. However, it would clearly be strange for Nordic nations to stay outside the most important enterprise for European peace and cooperation in modern history, and even stranger for them to abstain from taking an active part in shaping the future security order of Europe. In addition, living close to a former empire in painful transformation will present peace-time problems of such magnitude that it would be unwise for small neighbouring states not to try and counter such hazards within the wider framework of the EC.

It would be unsettling for Norway as a member of NATO not to be part of the European pillar of the alliance, and to have to make do with no more than associate membership of the Western European Union (WEU). For Finland and Sweden, which still retain the policy of remaining outside military alliances, EC membership represents a kind of political deterrence to any future would-be aggressor.

Present EC members understandably ask what attitude applicant countries will take to the Common Foreign and Security Policy (CFSP) within the emerging European Union. Finland and Sweden have, of course, accepted the Maastricht provisions, and they have no problems whatsoever with the measures under consideration for the CFSP. It goes without saying that they are no more able than today's EC members to define their position regarding steps towards a common defence policy or a common defence which might be proposed at some future date within the Union. But they are certainly well aware of the ultimate objectives of the Union and its CFSP.

As for Sweden, its people are only gradually realising how fundamentally the traditional parameters of Swedish security policy have changed. The reason is fairly obvious. During the Cold War, the Swedish government took every opportunity to emphasise the favourable security situation of Northern Europe compared to Central Europe. There were no massive standing forces in the region, no confrontational border between the alliances, and no focus for crises as was Berlin. Thus, it was not in Sweden's interest to engage in security cooperation with Central Europe. Instead, Sweden's task was to maintain a well-defended, non-aligned buffer area to ease Finland's position towards Moscow and contribute to a state of relatively low tension in the region.

This line of argument was actually quite correct, even if sometimes presented in sanctimonious terms. The Swedish public was all the more easily convinced as the reasoning conformed to their traditional beliefs and experiences. Further, it facilitated a certain brand of non-aligned idealism that appealed to most Swedes.

Now, however, it is dawning upon the Swedes that their security calculation is reversed in a Europe where Russia is closer to Sweden than to the continentals, and that internationalism can only start by contributing to the solving of problems in Europe.

Thus, self-interest and idealism will slowly but inexorably move Sweden towards supporting an effective and expanding CFSP. The same applies even more to the Finns. They have seldom been able to afford the luxury of caring that much for faraway nations, and their neutrality never developed any significant tinge of globalist ambition.

The WEU and NATO

Does this mean that Finland and Sweden will try to enter the WEU and NATO? Membership to the WEU will be an option only when they have joined the European Union (i.e., not before 1995). While Norway as a NATO member will enter the WEU as a matter of course, the issue is a different one for non-NATO states, for reasons too obvious to elaborate. This point is kept very much in mind by some present WEU and NATO members. Thus, Finland and Sweden will not take a decision until the role of the WEU and its relationship to NATO has been clarified as much as possible.

With regard to NATO membership, the Swedish government has said that no doors should be shut and no options excluded as the new European security order develops. The Finnish Foreign Ministry has been more explicit, particularly in a statement in February 1993. If there were to be a new polarisation of a Cold War nature in Europe, it said, Finland would have to consider whether it would need the deterrence of an alliance membership in order to strengthen its defence. The thrust of the statement, however, was that the issue is not topical and that Finland wants to support Russia's reform policies by promoting external stability. An extension of NATO membership to Finland and Sweden, it was added, would probably force the Western alliance to include the Visegrad states as well.

If this analysis is accepted, it is possible that Finnish and Swedish interests would at present best be served by keeping NATO's circle of members as it is. Drawing new lines in Europe's security terrain is a risky business. In particular, a line which would include some new states, but not the Baltic ones, might be interpreted in an undesirable way.

Further, as long as a resurgent Russian threat cannot be excluded, it is paramount to Finland and Sweden that the credibility and efficacy of NATO is not reduced. The inclusion of any new members should be viewed with this in mind. If, on the other hand, Western confidence-building cooperation with Russia is successful, it would seem wise not to rekindle the Russian exclusion syndrome. Would it not be better to focus on extending cooperation with Moscow, with the ultimate aim of including one day not only the countries presently discussed as possible NATO members, but also a Russia that has achieved a stable transformation to democracy and market economy? This goal, of course, presupposes that NATO could be transformed into the military arm of a Euro-Atlantic system of collective security, capable of preventing conflict between its own members as well as with states outside the system.

It has to be admitted, though, that this discussion is rather far-fetched and theoretical in view of the security challenges which face decision-makers in today's Europe. Containing crises of the kind seen in the former Yugoslavia is the foremost task. Whether a state is a member of the WEU or NATO, or both, has proved to be irrelevant when it comes to contributing to European efforts to curb the violence in Bosnia. Sweden, for instance, is preparing to send some 800 soldiers to protect the Tuzla safe area, which is more than some larger WEU or NATO member-states have so far been willing to contemplate.

Returning to the residual East–West dimension, it should be stressed again that NATO and the American commitment to the defence of Norway remain vitally important to Finland and Sweden. NATO extends a powerful stabilising influence on the entire Nordic region.

This plain truth was seldom, if ever, stated in public by Finnish or Swedish officials during the Cold War. This changed in 1989–90. However, the Norwegians have not had much time to savour the vindication of their NATO membership after the collapse of the Soviet Union. New apprehensions have emerged.

Norway and Denmark
The Norwegian worries about signs of decreased US and Western European interest in the High North may serve to illustrate, once again, the tension between hopes and fears in Nordic minds.

On the one hand, the Norwegians have seized upon the prospects for cooperation with Russia. They would like to use the riches of the Barents Sea as a basis for commercial ties with the Russians, while also attracting resources and investment from EC countries. The Norwegians share the same concern as the Finns and the Swedes about a spill-over from Russian disorder, primarily environmental degradation.

On the other hand, even with Russia's new political orientation, and even with the swift decline of Russia's military might, the Norwegians cannot fail to note a number of potentially unpleasant developments in terms of traditional security concerns.

The Strategic Arms Reduction Talks (START) Treaty will give increased relative weight to the submarine-based leg of Russia's strategic nuclear forces. This means that the Kola bases, and their protection, will continue to be important to Moscow as long as Russia maintains the ambition to remain a nuclear superpower. At the same time, under a cooperative relationship with Russia the US may not fully retain its traditional interest in the northern waters. Future American maritime strategy has not yet crystallised. Other more important global commitments may divert US naval resources from the Norwegian Sea.

NATO's transatlantic sea lines of communication depend upon the forward defence zone in the Norwegian and Barents Seas. However, with the decline of Russian naval forces this concern may not be felt as strongly as previously, and the priority given to the defence of Norwegian territory may accordingly be downgraded. Some Western European countries may perhaps be prepared to take on increased military responsibilities in Norway. But neither Germany nor the UK has the will nor the capability to replace the US commitment. Norwegian defence strategy is based upon early allied reinforcements, while the present trends in NATO are to increase flexibility and reduce earmarked reinforcements.

As Johan Jörgen Holst observed several years ago, Norway, from its position close to the northern ice-cap, has a different perspective from that of its allies. It is now the only NATO state which borders the Russian Federation. The resource boundary in the Barents Sea, stretching from the Norwegian–Russian border towards the North Pole, remains to be settled. In fact, this is the last unsolved border issue of any importance between Eastern and Western Europe.

To enumerate such uncertainties is not to deny the obvious fact that Norway's security position has very substantially improved over the last few years. It is rather to indicate the reasons why the Norwegians are so intent on ensuring strong security ties in the Atlantic as well as the continental direction. The recent rearrangement of NATO's command structure in north-western Europe will link Norway firmly to the Atlantic sea powers, while substantially weakening Norway's connection to Germany and Denmark. Yet, various ties to continental NATO states have been retained or set up under the new structure, and these have been deemed satisfactory.

The new command structure confirms Denmark's position within the defence orbit of Germany, but it is doubtful whether the new arrangement will make much difference. It will possibly underline

Denmark's domestic need to project even more clearly its determination to retain the US connection and the NATO framework of its security policy. NATO membership has never had stronger support in Danish public opinion. With the WEU, however, the Danish government has opted for no more than observer status. Even though Denmark subscribes to the CFSP, it has been exempted from participating in decisions with security-policy consequences.

Foreign observers may be tempted to read into all this an echo of Denmark's historical problems with Germany. It is indeed striking that while the question of the WEU is difficult, the Danes had no domestic problems when choosing, in the 1992 defence decision, to organise an international brigade (4,500 men) for peacekeeping or peace-enforcement missions. On the other hand, it remains a fact that decades ago Denmark and the Federal Republic pioneered military integration in the defence of Schleswig-Holstein and the Jutland peninsula. It might even be said that the Eurocorps concept was in a sense first put into practice by the Danes and the Germans, and that this was fully accepted long ago by Danish public opinion. To the extent that the Danes have 'a German problem' it is no more than an undercurrent, and there is no logic to what brings such emotions to the surface.

The Baltic states and Russia
The independence of the Baltic states was re-established and internationally recognised in late August and early September of 1991. In Baltic capitals, there has been one overriding objective with regard to security policy: the withdrawal of former Soviet forces from their territories. Understandably, until the Baltic states achieve full control of their territories, they see no reason to be very explicit about their plans for the future. It is clear, however, that they all want to be integrated into Western organisations, while avoiding any special relationship with Russia.

In their dealings with Russia they carry different burdens. In Estonia and Latvia, about a third of the population consists of post-war Russian immigrants, whose interests the Russian government feels entitled to protect. In Lithuania, where Soviet colonisation policies were much less brutal, Russian immigrants make up no more than 9% of the population, and it has been possible to grant automatic citizenship without running serious risks. For Vilnius, the burden may prove to be Russian transit rights to the Kaliningrad enclave.

This entity, with some 930,000 inhabitants and a surface area half as large as Belgium's, is a unique phenomenon in today's Europe. There are obvious questions about its viability, but even thornier ones about every conceivable alternative. Relatively soon, Russian decisions on military resource allocations to Kaliningrad may indicate the current perception in Moscow of Russia's security interests in the Baltic Sea region, now that their bases in the Baltic states have been, or will soon be, evacuated.

From the point of view of the Nordic states, the task of contributing to stability, prosperity and democracy in the region can only be approached in the wider context of parallel support to Russia. Their 'near Russia' is its north-western parts: the city and oblast of St Petersburg; the Karelian republic; and the Murmansk, Arkhangelsk, Novgorod, Pskov and Kaliningrad oblasts. For Sweden, support for the Baltic states will always claim the better part of available resources. But it is crucial that 'near Russia' acquires a real stake in maintaining a cooperative relationship with the Nordic states. This should be seen in the light of the Nordic aim to promote as much understanding between the Baltic states and their Russian neighbours as is feasible under the circumstances.

The Nordic states have only 23m inhabitants, compared to 8m in the Baltic states and some 15m in 'near Russia'. It goes without saying that the efforts of the Nordic states can only be effective as part of wider Western European endeavours. The challenge to overcome the division of Europe cannot be neatly compartmentalised in geographic terms, even though it is natural to focus on the areas closest at hand.

The consolidation of Baltic independence must begin by setting up effective instruments to exercise basic control of territory. 'Sovereignty support' is the term chosen for assistance with training and equipment for customs and border control, police forces, surveillance of territorial waters and air space. Naturally, much of this also serves the Nordics' interest of placing an effective screen between themselves and Russian *mafiosi*.

The Nordic countries have been quite reticent when it comes to provision of weapons for the fledgling armed forces of the Baltic states. This may change when Russian troop withdrawals have been completed. In any case, however, it will be a matter of small quantities. The Baltic states themselves seem very aware that their main defence against serious aggression must be political. One reason is geography and topography. Denmark and the Netherlands could not be defended effectively against Germany in 1940; the same logic applies to even smaller Russian neighbours in the 1990s. Another reason is cost: strong defence forces would entail expenses which could jeopardise economic development. The first line of defence is economic success, in particular for countries with large communities of immigrants from the adjoining power. On the other hand, there are the moral imperatives of any nation; and there is the historical evidence that only those who resist will impose the political costs that may deter an aggressor. The Baltic defence plans published so far seem to strike the right balance between these considerations.

The underlying problem in the Russo-Baltic relationship seems to be the two positions that Moscow still holds. One is that the Russian Federation, the Russian nation, or individual Russians should not be held responsible for past Soviet actions or have to suffer the consequences of these actions. The second is that the Soviet occupation and annexation of the Baltic states in 1940 was not really illegal. While the latter position is clearly untenable, the former raises much more complex issues to which there are not always easy answers. Together, these two positions make it possible for Russia to argue that retired Soviet officers should be allowed to stay on in Baltic cities, even in houses once confiscated from their owners, and that Russian immigrants who moved to the Baltic republics in the 1970s should be automatically granted Estonian or Latvian citizenship.

It will take time for the Russian and Baltic perspectives on these emotional issues to begin to converge. It will require much tact and common sense from both sides to handle concrete problems while the process of psychological adaptation goes on. Realistically, one has to be prepared for situations in which institutions like the Conference on Security and Cooperation in Europe (CSCE) or the Council of Europe will again be called upon to contribute.

There are, however, reasons for optimism. It is true that official Russian thinking in terms of special rights in their 'near abroad' is on the increase. Still, considering the extent of retreat from Soviet imperial positions which the Russian people has accepted over the last four years, it has to be acknowledged that no nation in modern history has acquiesced in such withdrawal with so little chauvinistic protest. It is further true that in the Baltic states there are radicals who would like to increase a feeling of insecurity among Russian immigrants in order to induce them to return to Russia. Yet, these radicals are remarkably few, considering the deprivations of 50 years of occupation. In fact, no other nations in modern history have freed themselves from similar foreign rule without killing a single agent of the occupying power.

Relations between very great and very small powers are never without problems. But it should not be beyond human achievement to reach an accommodation between a great nation that has succeeded in managing so much wrenching change with so little violence, and three small nations with such an outstanding record of civilised behaviour. They do share some positive experiences: common reformist struggle against the Soviet system in 1988–91, and during the last decades of the Tsars before 1914, when Russian rule was fairly benign to the

Baltic states and brought access to the remarkable culture of St Petersburg in those days. It remains a heartening fact that, despite recurrent crises, the separation has so far proceeded remarkably well.

European Security in a Wider World

PROFESSOR MASASHI NISHIHARA

Introduction

Today, European security has lost much of its salience in the wider global context. Gone is the import of the 'central balance' and the 'transatlantic bargain'. With the end of bipolar military and ideological tensions, the rest of the world, including the United States, no longer sees Europe as having a critical impact upon its own security. 'In the post-Cold War era, Europe looks set to become just one centre among several,' as European analysts argue.[1]

It is true that the conflict in Bosnia is a grave issue, showing little sign of peaceful or humanitarian solution. Yet the Bosnian question is confined to a 'small part' of Europe. Although the conflict could spread to the whole Balkan peninsula, as it did in the past, it is not likely to cause a Third World War – at least for the time being – because major external powers are unlikely to clash over the issue.

Western Europe, which used to be regarded as a rich, stable sub-area of Europe, now struggles with soaring social tensions such as urban crime stemming largely from unintegrated immigrants from the Third World. Western Europe has to carry the enormous burden of assisting the economy and, to a great extent, even the security of the rest of Europe. In this regard, Europeans are more preoccupied with their own affairs and thus are more inward-looking than before.

That Europe lives in an interdependent world, however, suggests that while it is important to identify the way in which European security can affect the security of the rest of the world in the post-Cold War period, it is also useful to discuss how European security may be influenced by changes taking place outside the continent. Just how Europe will be affected by these changes will depend upon its ability to manage their impact. Are Europeans capable of recognising the importance of these changes and responding to them? Europeans have to recognise this two-way flow of influence and to demonstrate that this continent can define and play a new security role in a wider world.

The external impact of European security

In post-Cold War Europe there are two contending security trends led by integrative and disintegrative forces: multilateral cooperation, as exemplified by the restoration of the Western European Union (WEU) and the formation of the North Atlantic Cooperation Council (NACC); and ethnic nationalism or self-assertion, as seen in the Bosnian turmoil. Both trends have important implications for global security. Multilateral dialogue on a region-wide basis helps prevent potential conflicts from developing into armed strife. NACC can help contain the mutual hostilities of potential adversaries within it, such as Russia and Ukraine and Hungary and Romania. At the same time, ethnic self-assertion has split Czechoslovakia into two states and is driving the former Yugoslavia into chaos.

If Europe, whose eastern geographical boundary remains unclear,[2] were able to manage its own security problems, such as the Bosnian crisis, it would set a model for the rest of the world. However, if Europe – which sends three permanent members to the United Nations (UN) Security Council – fails to solve its own security problems, the impact on the rest of the world will be negative.

Another important question that may arise if Europe cannot solve its own security problems is the efficacy of the North Atlantic Treaty Organisation (NATO). There will be a growing argument that NATO may not be suitable for dealing with ethnic conflicts. This kind of argument, in turn, may raise doubts about the efficacy of other US-led security treaties, including that of the US–Japan Security Treaty. Despite the fact that issues in the Korean peninsula will be quite different from those in Europe, critics may call for a review of the Treaty more strongly in the future than today.

If Western Europe should become an unstable area, for example, by failing to contain a strong, self-assertive Germany, European political cooperation or the WEU, not to mention NATO, may collapse. An unstable Western Europe would be a serious source of concern because it would probably fail to offer economic support or fail to help settle regional conflicts in the rest of Europe, and because many countries depend upon Western Europe for economic interactions. Such a Europe would also have a negative impact on the international economic system of which it is a key pillar.

External challenges to European security

Turning now to the question of external threat sources to European security today, it is difficult to identify direct external military threats. However, if security is seen in more than just military terms, there are several factors that may undermine European security. Many of these constitute indirect, but significant sources of threat.

The environment of European security will be affected by changes in major power configurations, in regional stability and in the international system. Naturally, these changes are interrelated. This paper will consider these changes in Europe, Russia and its southern neighbours, the Middle East and North Africa, the Asia–Pacific region and the international system.

US–RUSSIAN DISENGAGEMENT FROM EUROPE

During the Cold War era, Europe's security strategy was 'to keep Americans "in", Russians "out" and Germans "down"'. In the post-Cold War era, the Russians are practically 'out' and Americans are 'in', but half out. However, the Germans are not 'down', but they have contained themselves. (The problem of Germany will not be discussed here since it is an internal European issue.)

A planned reduction in US troop levels to 100,000 or so would narrow US military options in Europe and thus undermine the efficacy of NATO. The 'special relationships' between Washington and London and Washington and Bonn are eroding. US relations with France continue to be uneven. These new military developments would limit the scope of US diplomatic initiatives in Europe, as seen in the case of the Bosnian crisis, and the US is likely to be much less interventionist over European affairs than in the past.

Meanwhile, Russia, faced with its own economic collapse, has disengaged from Central and Eastern Europe. Although Russian arms may be being smuggled out to Serbian soldiers in Bosnia and Russian 'volunteers' may be being sent to support the Serbs, Russia cannot afford to take a stand openly hostile to the interests of Western European and American powers when Yeltsin depends so heavily on the West for his country's transition to a free market economy.

Washington's relative disengagement from Europe and Russia's substantial withdrawal from Central and Eastern Europe leave European countries with a greater responsibility for solving their own security problems. Under such circumstances the degree of US commitment to European security and the role that Russia may play in European affairs is critical.[3] If the US were not willing to play a substantial role in Europe, Europeans might find themselves in a difficult situation.

RUSSIA AND ITS SOUTHERN NEIGHBOURS

The collapse of the Soviet Union and the dissolution of the Warsaw Pact have significantly reduced the power and influence of Moscow. Moscow's power is now like it was in the eighteenth century. Western Russia is surrounded by new independent states (former Soviet republics) and Eastern European states which sit between it and Western

Europe, serving as a large buffer zone. Thus, for the time being, Russia's military threat to Europe has sharply declined.

Yet Russia today can still be a source of concern to European security: first, its agonies in the transition to a market economy may produce a large influx of economic refugees to Europe, particularly Germany. This inflow of refugees is likely to create social tensions which could undermine the stability of European societies. Second, Russia's poor management of environmental hazards, particularly nuclear power plants, nuclear waste and nuclear arms, worries Europeans. Chernobyl-type incidents can happen at any time, while the dumping of nuclear waste into the Arctic Ocean continues. Nuclear safety has become the nuclear threat in Europe. These social and environmental tensions are a source of concern, if not a direct threat, to European security.

What may constitute a more direct threat is the possibility of Russia's failure to democratise. The current stagnation in the democratisation process is being caused largely by 'political sabotage' on the part of those conservative members of parliament who resist the reforms being led by Boris Yeltsin. If a conservative anti-reformist government should emerge in Moscow, it could become hostile to Europe. Given such hostility, Russian nationalism could surge and tensions could arise between Russia and some of the former Soviet republics.[4] Unstable relations between Russia and its western and southern neighbours would arouse fears among Europeans.

THE 'ISLAMIC THREAT' FROM THE MIDDLE EAST AND NORTH AFRICA

The end of the Cold War nearly terminated the Russian role in the political and economic affairs of the Middle East and North Africa. The 1990–91 Gulf War was indicative of this. Conversely, the US has increased its influence, partly by acting as a catalyst for the Arab–Israeli peace talks, and partly by using the UN umbrella, under which it mobilised both European and moderate Arab nations to conduct the Gulf War against Saddam Hussein. The provisional autonomy granted to Jericho and Gaza for Palestinians in September 1993 was definitely a historical breakthrough for Middle East peace. However, signs of violent opposition by Islamic extremists remains formidable.

There are four factors in the region which may affect European security: first, the continuous inflow of legal and illegal migrants can aggravate the already high unemployment rate. Second, Islamic extremists continue to employ terrorist measures to promote their cause.[5] Four of the six countries which the US government designates as 'terrorist states' are from this region: Iran, Iraq, Syria and Libya.

Extremists in Iran, for instance, continue to express their willingness to assassinate Salman Rushdie, the British author who allegedly insulted Islam in his controversial book, *The Satanic Verses*. Third, oil-producing nations in the region may boycott the sale of oil to Europe, as they did in 1973. Fourth, hostile Islamic nations may deploy nuclear missiles and other advanced weapons to intimidate their European targets.

Not all of these factors present realistic concerns. For instance, Islamic nations would be unlikely to target with missiles European capitals where so many Muslim migrants live. Many Islamic nations would also think twice before deciding to boycott oil exports, for they too would suffer economically. Under the current global glut of oil the Arab boycott of oil will have less political and economic impact than in 1973.

Nonetheless, Islamic terrorist states threaten Europe by defying UN sanctions. Several Islamic countries hostile to Western interests have managed to survive Western-led UN sanctions. Suddam Hussein of Iraq continues to seek opportunities to defy UN sanctions; so does Libya.

TWO EMERGING ASIAN POWERS

The decline of overall Russian power and the relative decline of American economic might give room for two Asian powers to emerge as new players. Japan has already been a dominant economic competitor as well as partner for Europe. China has now emerged as a new economic giant.

A self-assertive Japan, having an export-oriented economy, may take a tougher stand on its trade and investment imbalance with the European Community (EC) than before, by refusing to make sufficient concessions. It may increase its share in the EC market, thus causing a higher rate of unemployment in Europe and weakening European economies. China's dynamic economic growth may overheat, but if it does not, an economically successful China could threaten Central and Eastern European economies since its products would probably compete with local products in European markets, thus damaging their economies and slowing the process of closing the gap between them and more competitive Western European markets. In this sense, both Japan and China present economic threats to Europe.

In more recent years, Japan has also begun to play a more active diplomatic role in the Asia–Pacific region than before. It coordinates with Washington and Seoul to put joint diplomatic pressure on Pyongyang to accept international inspections of its alleged nuclear development. It plays a major role in the peace process in Cambodia, and it has expressed its aspiration to serve on the UN Security Council as a permanent member. These developments suggest that Japan is becoming politically more self-assertive.[6]

China appears to regard such a Japan as a potential political competitor, one reason why it devotes much of its resources to the military build-up. Conversely, Japan and many East Asian countries are concerned about China's hegemonic ambitions.

China consistently denies its intention to become a hegemonic power. However, there are indications that it may become so, with its fast-growing economic capabilities allowing its military budget to increase at an impressive rate. Internal party and government papers apparently often claim that China should have strong military capabilities. China has a large potential for destabilising behaviour.[7] Such a power-conscious China could worsen relations with its neighbours, including Russia, Japan and India, and with the US.

The current trend points to the likelihood of Sino-Japanese rivalry. Under the present restrained relations between Tokyo and Moscow, the latter appears to favour its relations with Beijing. In fact, Moscow has recently sold some modern arms to China. But at the same time, Moscow–Beijing relations show growing signs of tension. The 'overpresence' of Chinese workers and traders in the Russian Far East has become a source of local tension. With crimes allegedly committed by Chinese on the increase, the Russian Internal Affairs Minister flew to the region recently to see for himself. In July, the Russian Pacific Fleet announced that it would dispatch its naval ships to the East China Sea to protect Russian commercial ships from being harassed and seized by Chinese naval patrol boats. Added to this is the speculation that the US may be taking more confrontational measures to dissuade China from secretly supplying missiles to potentially hostile nations such as Pakistan and Iran.

Whatever power configuration may emerge in the Asia–Pacific region, it may not pose a direct threat to Europe. However, if new political and military tensions should arise in the eastern part of Eurasia, Washington and Moscow will have to send more of their resources to that region than in the past, thus paying less attention to Europe.

CHANGES IN THE INTERNATIONAL SYSTEM

The current international economic system is one in which the Group of Seven (G-7) nations or the North play a dominant role. Constituting over 70% of the world's gross national product, the G-7 nations play a key part in maintaining the international monetary system, the General Agreement on Tariffs and Trade (GATT) trading system, and international trading institutions, among others. They occupy about 80% of the world's official development aid, and the end of the Cold War has enhanced their power.

The international system, however, continues to face two challenges. First, the smooth running of the system depends to a large extent on the stable supply of oil and other natural resources to the North for its industrial activities, and on the reasonable economic growth of the South. The economic stagnation in the Third World, which often leads to political instability and regional insecurity, can threaten the international system and Europe.

Second, the system also depends on the abilities of the G-7 to maintain the security of sea-lanes around the world in order to sustain trade. The US maintained a naval superiority during the Cold War and its naval role continues to be important. Today, Russia is hardly capable or willing to obstruct the sea-lanes, but they are still subject to harassment by pirates from smaller nations. Many important sea-lanes are also in areas of territorial disputes and are not completely free of danger.

The international security system is being strengthened by the efforts of the West to adopt tighter Nuclear Non-Proliferation Treaty (NPT) regulations, the Missile Technology Control Regime (MTCR) and the Chemical Weapons Ban Treaty. The system will be weakened if nuclear arms proliferate among potentially hostile nations, including North Korea, Iraq, Iran, Pakistan and Libya. Conventional arms also proliferate fast among the developing countries, thus constituting a new source of regional instability, which can directly affect European security.

When the composition of the permanent members of the UN Security Council changes the international security system may also change. If Japan and Germany become permanent members, they are members of the West which already plays a dominant part in the Security Council. However, if India, Nigeria, Egypt and Brazil, which are frequently quoted as candidates, should join the permanent membership, the nature of North–South relations may change, and the Security Council may not always function to favour European, particularly Western European, interests. The Security Council, for instance, may fail to pass resolutions imposing sanctions on those countries attempting to defy the arms-control regimes. This situation may adversely influence European security.

How should Europe cope with those external challenges?
'POWER' AND 'LINKS' APPROACHES
Europeans, who tend to be preoccupied with issues inside Europe, need not pay attention to those external sources of threat to European

security. These threats today are essentially indirect in nature, but they can become more direct, depending on circumstances. How should Europe cope with them?

To cope with these sources of threat, Europe should employ both a 'realpolitik' approach and an 'interdependency' approach, depending upon the sources of threat. These approaches will be called a 'power' approach and a 'links' approach, respectively. The first aims at playing a balance-of-power game and trying to accomplish favourable power relations; it is willing to confront hostile nations. The second approach aims at engaging all nations concerned, including potentially hostile nations, for regional cooperation and pre-emptive diplomacy. This approach attempts to build institutional links with those countries concerned.

If the three categories of threat described in this paper, namely, changes in major power configurations, changes in regional stability and changes in the international system, are to be used here, Europe should employ a skilful combination of the two approaches to each of the three categories. The basic guideline will be to use a 'power' approach where hostile powers are present, and to use a 'links' approach where only potentially hostile powers are present.

COPING WITH MAJOR POWER CONFIGURATIONS

Europe has to define its strategic interests in terms of what power configuration outside its own region would favour European security. It appears that, because of several uncertain factors in the former Soviet Union, it would still be essential for Europe to keep America 'in' and build up a new partnership with Washington.[8] If current disagreements between Russia and Ukraine, for instance, should develop into armed conflicts, can any European state intervene to stop them? The US can still play a vital role, although it may actually decide not to. Europe should be making a 'power' approach here and keep the US commitment to Europe, primarily through NATO, to deter regional armed conflicts.[9]

At the same time, Europe can certainly employ its diplomatic and economic means to help maintain the stability of international relations among the former Soviet republics and between Russia and Eastern European states. To do this, it already has important institutional links with the former Soviet republics, namely, through the Conference on Security and Cooperation in Europe (CSCE) and NACC. These links need to be strengthened in order to minimise the possibility of intra-NACC conflicts, such as between Russia and Ukraine.

The US is maintaining its naval superiority around the globe, and playing a key role in ensuring the security of the sea-lanes. For this reason as well, European–US, as well as US–Japanese, security relations are vital.

The emergence of Japan and China as major powers in Asia and their possible rivalry does not really affect European security. However, if such rivalry should develop into armed conflict, the US and Russia may be dragged in. It is in Europe's interest to help avert such a development. Thus Europe should take a 'power' approach here in an attempt to support Japan diplomatically and help balance China's military power. But at the same time, Europe should develop more institutional links with China, engaging it in security and political dialogue.

COPING WITH REGIONAL SECURITY

Those regions whose security is likely to affect Europe more directly will be Central Asia, the Middle East and North Africa. Enlarged Azeri–Armenian conflicts over the Nagorno-Karabakh area and Iraqi–Turkish conflict over the Kurds, for instance, can affect the security of Turkey, a member of NATO. Europe has to study carefully what its interests are and what means it should employ to pursue its interests. Although, generally speaking, Europe should adopt a 'power' approach here to support Turkey, it should also adopt a 'links' approach to the Central Eurasian region, for instance, by establishing contacts with the newly born Economic Cooperation Organisation (ECO).[10]

The Middle East and North African region is more crucial to European security. The issues for Europe include: terrorism, religious and cultural intolerance, migration and the proliferation of arms of mass destruction. European states have had different and often complicated relations with many countries in the region, frequently through colonial connections. Here again Europe should use both 'power' and 'links' approaches. It should employ a 'power' approach to deter hostile nations or 'terrorist' nations. Europe used a 'power' approach with Iraq during the Gulf War and is making a 'power' approach to Libya over the PanAm bombing of 1988. This is appropriate, for any power configuration in the Middle East and North Africa that will strengthen Iraq and Libya does not favour European security interests. Europe has to be involved in balancing these two countries, plus Iran and Syria, by supporting Israel and moderate Arab nations such as Saudi Arabia and Egypt.

At the same time, Europeans make efforts to bring about reconciliation between the Arabs and Israel, through political and intellectual dialogues and economic interaction. However, European attempts to help bring about peace in the region have not made much progress, although one of the few successful efforts has been to develop institutional links with moderate Islamic nations. They are the Arab–Maghreb Union through which southern Europeans have developed ties with moderate North African states, and the Gulf Cooperation Council (GCC), in which Saudi Arabia plays a key role and with which the EC established its institutional links.[11] Europe should consider establishing more of these links in the region.

An important question for Europe is whether NATO and the WEU can be mobilised to help maintain or restore the regional security in the Middle East and North Africa as well as Central Eurasia. These military roles cannot be overstretched, but they cannot entirely ignore, for instance, Turkey's request for NATO intervention in case regional turmoil starts to threaten Turkey's territorial integrity.

The security of the Asia–Pacific region may not be a direct concern for Europeans. However, if security is conceived broadly, the region's market is growing enormously and should affect European economy. Although Europe has many serious economic frictions with Japan, it also has many institutional links with it, such as the EC–Japan Council, the Organisation for Economic Cooperation and Development (OECD), G-7 summits and so on. By contrast, although Europe has started to have economic conflicts with China, it has so far not developed similar institutional links with it.

Political instability in the region could also affect the long trade route along the Pacific coast of the Asian continent, a route that suffers numerous territorial disputes. The EC has accomplished successful institutional links with the region:[12] it is a member of the annual Association of South-east Asian Nations (ASEAN) Post-Ministerial Conference, along with the US, Canada, Japan, South Korea, Australia and New Zealand, plus six ASEAN member-states. Europe can continue to strengthen these links.

COPING WITH CHANGES IN THE INTERNATIONAL SYSTEM

The international economic and political system that functioned during the Cold War was essentially the trilateral cooperation among Europe, North America and Japan. That cooperation served their respective strategic interests in coping with Soviet power and promoted free trade. The three regions suppressed their own economic grievances for the sake of protecting their overriding security interests. Today, with the disintegration of the Soviet Union, the three regions can afford to be in open competition with each other and make their mutual complaints public. The difficulty in reaching the Uruguay Round of the GATT talks illustrates this situation.

Yet it is in Europe's interests to maintain the current international system. Europe's close relations with Japan at the expense of the US would not serve its own interests, since it is the US, not Japan, that can help maintain security in Europe. Europe is still likely to retain fairly close relations with the US. There are many economic frictions between Japan and the US, but they are unlikely to break up their alliance. Japan and Europe can therefore loosen their relations, but here again it is in Europe's interests to be able to use Japanese money, for instance, for UN peacekeeping operations and for support of the Russian transition to a market economy. In fact, close European–US relations at the expense of Japan will make the Asian power feel isolated and may drive it to an independent course, as it did in the 1930s. The 'links' approach will avert the break-up of the trilateral cooperation and the current international system. That approach will help strengthen Europe's role.

Nonetheless, Europe's economic and political clout may decline as the Asia–Pacific region becomes economically stronger and as the Third World becomes more heavily armed. The decline of Europe may also be reflected in the widening of the Security Council's permanent membership, with the inclusion of non-European states such as Japan, India or Brazil. That would weaken the European influence in international politics. If Europe cannot resist the change in the composition of the Security Council, it can at least work to bring about a gradual change in its composition, so that the North and the South can adjust better to the change and enjoy more productive relations. As the Third World becomes richer, it will have more sophisticated arms. Europe, together with the US and Japan, has to work to arrest this trend. The 'links' approach will make cooperative engagement between the North and South more fruitful.

Conclusion

In the post-Cold War years Europe should redefine its security interests. External challenges to European security today are seen in more than just military terms, and most of them pose indirect rather than direct threats. These challenges will be affected by changes in major-power configurations, regional security and stability, and the international system. Europe needs to watch with care changes in the US commitment overseas, Russia and its southern neighbours, Japanese and Chinese powers, the stability of the Midddle East and North Africa, and the international system.

In coping with these external challenges, Europe should adopt a skilful combination of a 'balance-of-power' approach and an 'institutional links' approach. Europe should keep the American power 'in' and follow closely where Russia might go. It needs to look at the economic and political changes taking place in Central Eurasia, the Middle East and North Africa. Both the 'power' approach and 'links' approach are important. Europe has to consider how NATO and the WEU can be mobilised to help keep the peace in its neighbouring regions, the GCC and the Arab–Maghreb Union. The international system will change, as new powers join the Security Council's permanent membership and Europe should find ways to make gradual adjustment for it.

Notes

[1] Barry Buzan, et al., The European Security Order Recast: Scenarios for the Post-Cold War Era (London and New York: Pinter Publishers, 1990), p. 61.

[2] 'What are the Boundaries of Europe?' in ibid., pp. 45–49.

[3] John van Oudenaren, 'Central and Eastern Europe and the Former Soviet Union', in Nanette Gantz and John Roper (eds), Towards a New Partnership: US–European Relations in the Post-Cold War Era (Paris: WEU, 1993), pp. 13–34.

[4] Walter Laquer, 'Russian Nationalism', Foreign Affairs, vol. 70, no. 5, Winter 1991–92, pp. 104–16; and Dmitri K. Simes, 'America and the Post-Soviet Republics', Foreign Affairs, vol. 71, no. 3, Summer 1992, pp. 73–89.

[5] Judith Miller, 'The Challenge of Radical Islam', Foreign Affairs, vol. 72, no. 2, Spring 1993, pp. 43–56.

[6] Despite the fragility of his coalition government, Prime Minister Morihiro Hosokawa is likely to take an active, internationalist stand over Japan's role in UN peacekeeping operations, on Japanese–US security relations and the GATT Uruguay Round talks, among other things.

[7] David Shambaugh, 'China's Security Policy in the Post-Cold War Era', Survival, Summer 1992, p. 99.

[8] Gantz and Roper (eds), Towards a New Partnership.

[9] Charles L. Glaser, 'Why NATO is Still Best: Future Security Arrangements for Europe', International Security, vol. 18, no. 1, Summer 1993, pp. 550.

[10] The ECO was originally established in 1983 by non-Arab Islamic states, Turkey, Iran and Pakistan. In 1992 it was joined by five former Soviet republics, Azerbaijan, Turkmenistan, Uzbekistan, Tajikistan and Kyrgyzstan. Armenia, Romania and Afghanistan are also said to be considering joining.

[11] Elfriede Regelsberger, 'The Euro-Arab Dialogue: Procedurally Innovative, Substantially Weak', and Eberhard Rhein, 'Agreement with The Gulf Cooperation Council: A Promising If Difficult Beginning', in Geoffrey Edwards and Elfriede Regelsberger (eds), Europe's Global Links (London: Pinter Publishers, 1990), pp. 57–65 and 112–17, respectively.

[12] Manfred Mols, 'Cooperation with ASEAN: A Success Story', in Edwards and Regelsberger (eds), Europe's Global Links, pp. 57–65.

Forces and Alliances for a New Era

HON. LES ASPIN

A fundamental question dominated the work of the US Department of Defense in the first half of 1993. It has probably dominated the work of other nations' defence establishments as well, and is something that nations should consider together. The question is, what kind of armed forces does the US need in this new era? This will be addressed first from a national perspective, then in terms of how the US relates to European security.

For its part, the Department of Defense has just finished drawing up a comprehensive blueprint to restructure US military forces for the post-Cold War, post-Soviet era. The plan resulted from a 'start-from-scratch' process known as the 'Bottom-Up Review'.

This Review was undertaken from the bottom up in order to take account of the dramatic changes in the world. It is impossible to overestimate how the Soviet threat dominated US Cold War defence planning. It drove its defence budgets, tactics and doctrine. It even determined the design of US weapons. With the Soviet threat gone, what should the defence establishment be geared against now?

In the new era, America, and its allies and friends, face four new dangers: regional conflicts; the proliferation of nuclear and other weapons of mass destruction; threats to economic well-being; and the possible failure of democratic reform in the former Soviet bloc and elsewhere. These were the driving force behind the 'Bottom-Up Review'.

The dangers from regional, ethnic and religious conflicts do not put the existence of the US at risk, but they could threaten vital American interests, American friends, American allies and the standards of conduct they strive to strengthen.

As for the second danger – the threat of proliferation of weapons of mass destruction – the area of the former Soviet Union still contains thousands of nuclear weapons whose security may be at risk given the deterioration of the old mechanisms of control. Many people in the area have weapons-making knowledge and their expertise could reach the world market. Furthermore, nations hostile to freedom and democracy, like Iraq and North Korea, are determined to acquire nuclear weapons.

This greatly concerns the US, especially since more nations are developing ballistic missiles that can deliver weapons of mass destruction. While the threat of massive Soviet nuclear attack has subsided, the new nuclear danger stems from the prospect of terrorists or rogue states with a handful of nuclear weapons.

The third danger is the failure to see US national security interests, and those of its friends and allies, in a way that includes economic concerns. Economic well-being is vital to security. President Clinton's economic programme acknowledges this fundamental fact – the most important thing the US can do for its security over the long term is to strengthen its economy.

This is also true for the West as a whole. The Western Alliance must not fall prey to economic nationalism. It needs to sustain the economic vitality that has made the free-market approach the model for the world. So, it must work in autumn 1993 to conclude the Uruguay Round of trade negotiations in the General Agreement on Tariffs and Trade (GATT). Its failure could prolong global recession, breeding protectionism in the international market-place.

Danger four is the possibility that democratic reform will fail in the former Soviet Union, Central and Eastern Europe and elsewhere. The Soviet superpower threat may be in the past, but if dictatorships arise from the pieces, it would mean a less peaceful world and a more difficult world for all, as well as more expensive.

When these four dangers are added up it is clear that the whole threat picture has changed. During the Cold War, the US knew who its primary potential adversary was. It used to stare at that adversary across the Fulda Gap in Germany. Now it is looking at four lesser dangers, but it is not known precisely where they will emerge, or when. The 'Bottom-Up Review' considered the four new dangers and built a new strategy, force structure and defence policy, block by block. This new plan responds to the world as it is now developing.

But the four dangers also add up to one key conclusion – the US must, and shall, remain a world power in this new era. It is not going to withdraw from the world. It no longer needs to prepare for global war, but the dangers to its interests are still global. It must be prepared to deal with these dangers effectively, no matter where in the world they may emerge. The Review has spelled out what military forces and capabilities are needed to meet the four dangers.

Of the four dangers, the one that affects the issues of force size and structure the most is the requirement to deter and defeat major regional conflicts. The others also have some influence. The need to maintain a peacetime overseas presence will affect force size to some degree. The need to conduct smaller-scale operations and maintain nuclear deterrence will require special military capabilities. But when it comes to force planning, the most important part of US military strategy is the need to fight, and win, major regional conflicts.

Indeed, the US must field military forces that can fight and win two major regional conflicts, and nearly simultaneously. This decision is at the heart of its force-structure sizing. There are indeed potential regional aggressors – there could be more than one – that can threaten US interests, friends and allies. But does the US have to size its forces for two such conflicts? The answer is yes, and here are the reasons.

First, if forces are fighting in one major regional conflict, the US does not want a second potential aggressor to be tempted to launch an attack elsewhere in the world because he believes the United States cannot respond to an attack on an ally or friend. It can, and it will.

Second, a two-conflict strategy provides enough forces in case a future adversary, or coalition of adversaries, arises with a military force that is larger than today's potential aggressors. Thus, the two-conflict strategy gives a hedge against threats the US could confront 10–20 years from now. The post-Cold War world is dynamic and unpredictable, and the US must maintain military capabilities that are large enough and flexible enough to cope with unforeseen threats.

It has designed its forces to support this 'win-win' military strategy – that is, forces that, together with those of its allies in a threatened region, can fight and win two nearly simultaneous major regional conflicts. But these forces can also support other coalition operations: peacekeeping, peace enforcement and humanitarian assistance. The forces will be lean, highly flexible, highly mobile, and able to deploy quickly in a crisis. They will increase the international community's ability to respond to crises rapidly and effectively.

Three points flow from this. Point number one is about the criticality of allied cooperation. Point two, the criticality of force enhancements to enable the US to execute its win-win strategy. The third point addresses the broader issue of European security.

The US is restructuring its military forces to face the dangers of the new era. But that does not mean it ought to confront the dangers alone. These are mutual dangers. The American public will see this clearly and will want a mutual response. The contributions of its coalition partners are crucial, as they were in *Operation Desert Storm*. Years of experience in the North Atlantic Treaty Organisation (NATO) of working and training together paid off: NATO had prepared the West for coalition warfare. This is one of the reasons why the Atlantic Alliance is still so vital.

But the end of the Cold War has changed the way the West must plan coalition operations. During the Cold War years, US planning focused on a NATO response to Warsaw Pact aggression in Europe. It knew who would fight alongside it; it knew what roles each would play in combined operations; and it conducted combined military exercises to prepare for Soviet-led aggression.

All this has changed. Yet there must still be preparations for combined US–European operations. In many areas where mutual interests may be threatened, however, there is no formal alliance structure. That is, there are no arrangements that determine in advance which nations will join against certain threats, when they will join, with what forces, and for what missions.

This needs to be changed. The West must work together to ensure military cooperation in areas that are critical to shared interests. It must develop military partnerships – in NATO and elsewhere – to thwart the new dangers faced not only in Europe, but elsewhere. As part of this goal, a top priority for the US at the NATO summit in January 1994 was to continue the process of restructuring and refocusing NATO in order better to meet the dangers of the post-Cold War era.

To deal with two major regional contingencies nearly simultaneously, the US capability must be enhanced. The United States determined two things. First, it expects regional aggressors to be well-armed. Second, it must be prepared for these aggressors to launch an armour-heavy offensive against the outnumbered forces of a neighbouring state, and do it at short notice.

The key to dealing with this kind of aggression in the win-win strategy is a series of force enhancements. Two areas are particularly critical. The first is mobility – the US needs to deliver its forces to distant battle areas and sustain them there. The second is war-fighting capability – it needs to be able to halt an invasion or stop an aggressor during the crucial first phase of battle.

Mobility assets. The US plans to add new military aircraft and new roll-on, roll-off sea-lift ships to strengthen its ability to send combat forces, particularly heavy ground forces, oversees quickly.

War-fighting capability. It wishes to improve its early-arriving combat power to halt invading forces in the first phase of conflict. This involves a number of enhancements.

First, it will position more Army heavy-brigade equipment sets ashore overseas – two sets of equipment in South-west Asia; one or two in the Pacific; plus another afloat that could be sent to either region. It also plans to keep five heavy Army brigade sets and one Marine brigade set in Europe.

Second, it is pursuing new technologies that can give more punch on the battlefield. These include 'smart' anti-armour weapons for early-arriving air, land and sea forces – Army missiles and helicopters, Air

Force bombers and Navy strike aircraft, for example. These weapons can put a large number of armoured vehicles out of service quickly. To make full use of these weapons, the US is also pursuing integrated modern battlefield surveillance to detect the main concentrations of enemy forces, process and analyse the data, and pass it to the 'shooters' before it becomes obsolete.

Third, faster deploying carrier-based air power is being introduced. During conflicts, the number of strike aircraft and air crews on early-arriving carriers will be increased to strengthen their firepower.

Fourth, more Marines are needed. Under the defence programme the Clinton administration inherited, the Marine Corps end strength was set to decline to 159,000 active-duty troops. Now the Marines will be kept at 174,000. This will provide more ready and capable Marine Expeditionary Forces.

With these enhancements, the US is confident that its armed forces will be able to fight and win two nearly simultaneous major regional conflicts. But perhaps the most important force enhancement is the commitment by friends and allies to face the post-Cold War conflicts and challenges together.

That leads to the third point – what all of this means for European security.

The US has important long-standing ties with Europe. The two share common values, objectives and policies and have cooperated as allies and friends for years. None of this will change. In fact, it is even more important as the post-Cold War dangers and challenges are faced together. European security is American security.

The most concrete example of US commitment to European security is the US forces deployed there. It plans to retain about 100,000 troops in Europe to the end of the decade, even as its overall troop levels are coming down.

However, public support for a US troop presence in Europe cannot be taken for granted. It hinges on how relevant NATO remains, and to remain relevant NATO's forces must be able to respond to the challenges of the new era. These include the challenges of peacekeeping and peace-enforcement operations. But NATO forces must also be prepared to deter and defeat aggression against Western interests beyond the NATO boundaries.

The Atlantic Alliance has been crucial to the West's security for more than four decades. It can continue to be crucial by seizing new opportunities to advance mutual interests.

The US has just reviewed its defence needs. It has re-examined the contribution it can make to collective security. Many nations are engaged in similar reviews. Together, the West must adjust its defence plans and programmes to the dangers and challenges of the new era.

Conclusion

DR BO HULDT

In his introductory plenary address on 'European Unity and European Security', M. Jacques Delors presented a background analysis based on four points.

First, security remains an issue of utmost relevance, but perceptions of adversaries, confrontation and cooperation have changed dramatically.

Second, non-military aspects of security are more important than ever. Problems of international development are now evident and the European Community (EC) is a proponent of soft security to promote economic growth and welfare.

Third, a new world order – interdependence – and a global society which limit national sovereignty are now emerging.

Fourth, and perhaps most important here, the EC needs to act swiftly and decisively to meet these new challenges.

For the EC to act, it must develop the political will and a new strategy and provide for joint action, which includes providing appropriate military resources. Partnership – within the framework of an emerging European security identity – and cooperation between all security institutions are vital to safeguard common interests. This involves the development of a European Defence Community, still a project in *statu nascendi,* but a definite concept nonetheless.

In his response to M. Delors, Jim Steinberg expressed doubts about whether such a widened community would really strengthen the European security system.

He also expressed concerns about the barbarians not at the gate – in Bosnia or wherever – but rather inside the citadel or in the heart of Western Europe itself – pointing to the corrosive forces now at work there, such as political extremism and racism. Both the situation in the former Yugoslavia and the long tug of war over the Maastricht Treaty indicate the West's various deficiencies, fears and doubts. The failure over the former Yugoslavia is not a failure of the West's institutions, that hapless architecture, but of its willingness to use them.

The subsequent debate, or the 'dialogue' as Delors phrased it, took the form of an open and straightforward seminar discussion between the speaker and a number of conference participants, including diplomats questioning Delors' proposed European Defence Community (and the role of the Commission therein), upholding the new North Atlantic Treaty Organisation (NATO) mandate – which is certainly no longer East–West – and expressing concerns over too much 'French-ness'. It was also observed, by a well-known Harvard professor, that the soft security offered by the Community to the Eastern European countries in the shape of high tariffs and economic non-access, as well as delays in discussing proposed membership, might be improved upon. There were also discussions on sovereignty and the role of the EC in upholding, selectively or without compromise, fundamental freedoms and human rights. A request was made for direct support for Bosnia, to which Delors replied by referring to 'the shame of the Community' for not having taken action, and restating the activist views he has consistently expressed for some three years.

Professor Peter Frank introduced the other half of Europe in his plenary address on 'Stability and Instability in Eastern Europe', by first pointing to the historical relationship between a Central and Eastern Europe uncomfortably sandwiched between Germany and Russia. The key to European security, the *necessary*, but not *sufficient* condition for European security today and tomorrow, is Russia; Germany does not, at this point in time, present similar problems. Russia, however, is a state in acute crisis – economic, political, constitutional, social and moral. A crucial question, with roots in Russian history and debate, is whether the country can really be rebuilt, or whether only by destroying it can it be saved. While the West likes to think that Russia now looks Westwards for its models, patterns and contacts, Professor Frank moved Eastwards after discussing the Russian constitutional issues by way of the crucial relationship between Moscow and the ex-Soviet republics. The East denotes the Central Asian border where Russia now holds the front between Tajikistan and Afghanistan, a 1,300 kilometre-wide Thermopylae against Islam – or so some in Moscow appear to see it.

Russia's uncertainty about whether to be European, that is 'Western', Atlanticist or Euro-Asian, is still there – a matter undecided, and perhaps unlikely to be decided quickly. Catherine Kelleher as respondent saw reason for a certain, or rather potential, optimism. A challenging analogy was made comparing the present problems of Russian constitutional and centre-periphery relations, and the US of the 1830s during the Andrew Jackson presidency with, no doubt, 'Our union – it must be preserved' as the relevant point of reference. (I must confess that I had never before thought of Rhuslan Khasbulatov as a Russian version of John C. Calhoun!) The respondent strongly underlined the need to see Russia as a partner and that it really is the West which holds the key to European security through the way it now reacts to the former East.

In the subsequent debate, Sergei Blagovolin spoke for a Russian, specific version of democracy and revealed himself as only a moderate destructionist: it is the political culture, not the 'country', that must be destroyed. Again it was made clear that while stability and progress in Russia will not in itself make for European security, without that stability there can be no European security.

Ukraine was introduced into the debate with a representative expressing deep concern over the Russian approach to the 'near abroad' and its direct threats to former Soviet republics; whether such direct threats, even of war, had been made by the Russian side in the recent negotiations between Presidents Kravchuk and Yeltsin over the Black Sea Fleet became a subsequent bone of contention.

The Islamic threat, however, was rejected by a spokesman for that civilisation and Robert Blackwill dampened hopes of Russian willingness to see things the Western way by presenting a long list of grievances, suspicions and unhappiness among Russian generals about US and Western mediation and interference in Russian affairs, and the possible extension of NATO to the gates of Russia. The discussion ended with the recognition of Russia's great disillusion with the West and the food for thought this offered to those Western countries which believe themselves to be actively supporting Russia – and thus expect Russian responses and good behaviour accordingly.

The third plenary was dedicated to 'NATO's Role in a Changing Europe'. 'The collapse of Soviet communism has left the West with a paradox: there is less threat, but also less peace', said Secretary-General Manfred Wörner. This new situation must now be faced both in terms of costs – what is the West willing to pay for security in this new European setting? – and in terms of resolve. Shortcomings on the Bosnian crisis were summed up without pity. Future effective crisis management will have to build on the lessons learned about intervention, consistency of purpose and seriousness of intent. For the future, NATO remains the key actor in cooperation with the United Nations (UN) in its new role as crisis manager. There has been failure in Bosnia, but this is more a result of not having used the instrument at hand (in this case NATO) than of this same instrument's failure to function. The challenges for the future can be seen in terms of providing stability, resolving crises and conflicts, maintaining the transatlantic relationship and preventing Europe's relapse into old-style nationalism, balance-of-power coalition-building and fragmentation. The Atlantic Alliance has provided stability, the conditions for European welfare and community-building; without this transatlantic link there would be neither NATO, nor the EC nor, for that matter, a modernising East integrated into Europe. NATO must now play its role in stabilising Europe, which requires it to project stability to the East and widen the Alliance to Central and Eastern Europe without isolating any European state. NATO is not a closed shop. It will also have a more pronounced European role.

In his response to Dr Wörner's speech, François Heisbourg spoke in favour of caution on the issue of widening NATO ('where do you draw the line?') and highlighted the importance of shared strategic interests and perspectives rather than institutional approaches which in themselves are no substitute for strategic thinking. The concern should be with security goals and functions. In the subsequent debate, questions were put to Dr Wörner both about the possible future place in NATO for the former Warsaw Pact countries, which, according to Wörner, would for the time being have to console themselves with the North Atlantic Cooperation Council (NACC), and about what to do in Bosnia. Wörner restated his personal view that decisive action was needed in Bosnia, but added that the West could not afford to fail if it did act.

The question to which the then US Secretary of Defense Les Aspin addressed himself in his plenary presentation was what kind of armed forces are needed in the post-Cold War era. The old threat of a major war between East and West has fragmented into four new dangers: regional conflicts; proliferation of nuclear weapons and weapons of mass destruction; threats to US economic well-being; and the possible failure of democratic reforms in the former Soviet bloc or elsewhere. It must, of course, be observed that these threats do not all lend themselves to military solutions – a General Agreement on Tariffs and Trade (GATT) impasse is hardly manageable through military intervention. It might also be said that these threats are not all new and did exist in some shape during the Cold War. What is new is that regional conflicts – and not the imminent danger of a catastrophic confrontation between East and West – will now determine the size and structure of forces. Not only that, however; the future will supposedly be characterised by security arrangements in various parts of the world in the shape of 'partnerships'. The over-arching issue is thus less the exact number of weapons, aircraft carriers and divisions than the character of the political and strategic alliances and agreements that will serve to prevent and pre-empt regional conflicts. That Europe is a part of this the West knows, as well as the fact that after the Cold War it might be even more important than before for Europe and the US to face the new dangers together.

This now looks essential against the background of pessimistic views on US troop withdrawals, a widening Atlantic and worries that the burden of proof regarding the US presence in Europe may now have shifted from those who argue for US withdrawal to those who thought it demonstrated once and for all that the US presence in Europe is in the interests of both Europeans and Americans.

In his comments, Professor Sir Michael Howard was happy to concur that European security is American security, but he also put the question 'What are the boundaries of the Europe with which you identify?'. He expressed some concern over US plans to repeat the Gulf War. Such conflicts are not expected to occur in any great number, and minor ones, calling for lower-level but long-term responses, are more likely scenarios for the future. 'Duresse' rather than 'masse' would be called for. How did the US see the role of the allies in this context? In reply, Secretary Aspin agreed with the latter scenario, but stated that the more challenging task (i.e., Gulf War-type conflicts) must be planned for, while the same forces could be used in smaller numbers for minor contingencies.

In his responses to Sir Michael and to questions from the floor, Secretary Aspin underlined that the mandate and role of NATO would have to be discussed further among the Allies, that US forces in the future could and would be placed under the command of nationals from other countries, that the US would still want to maintain a unilateral right to decide if and when it should go to war and to act alone when US security interests were directly threatened – although the overall importance of US allies in regional conflicts was truly great; in the Gulf War, Allied support had been indispensable and the US needs its allies, politically and militarily. Secretary Aspin also predicted, at some point in the future, a new look at nuclear issues, not only the Nuclear Non-Proliferation Treaty (NPT), but also the whole 'theology' of nuclear weapons in the post-Cold War setting.

Committee 1, dealing with 'European Security in the 1990s – Issues and Agenda', was intended as a meeting place for academic analysts and practitioners to discuss the whole catalogue of woes and possibilities, focusing on substance, but also on approaches and concepts. The idea was to examine the changing security agenda and to suggest tasks for the strategic studies community (specifically for the IISS research agenda).

The paper prepared by Professor Lawrence Freedman presents the now melancholy case for the strategic studies of yesterday, with containment and stability the key words and the new challenges, with an emphasis on rapid change and system transformation. Resistance to the new conditions of strategic studies has been reflected in the obsession with 'architecture' and the ambition to build a system even more stable than that of the Cold War. Disillusionment in 1992 with the problems of European unification, with the former Yugoslavia as the new defining conflict and with risks of instability and disintegration in Eastern Europe, has shifted this preoccupation with stability and structure to the consideration of processes which are much more difficult to handle. Faced with the contrary forces of European integration and disintegration, the West is also being invited to stand up to the moral challenge – in Freedman's words, 'am I doing the right thing?' Frustrations over the former Yugoslavia have made such soul-searching a matter of both private concern and professional self-criticism.

The Committee discussions revealed clear differences in perspective and approach among the academics and the practitioners. 'Theological' discussions were contrasted with the needs of the decision-makers to know what to do. One former policy-maker put it in concrete terms by asking 'under what conditions are we willing to send our soldiers out to die?', while a colleague wondered how academic discussions like these would have helped him two years ago when the situation in the former Yugoslavia started to become truly critical.

In general the views, not only on action or inaction in Bosnia, but also on future prospects for European security in a larger context, thus tended to differ: the practitioners, taking a shorter-term perspective, were rather optimistic about Europe managing; while the academics, taking a longer-term view, were more pessimistic, even to the point of suggesting that Europe may now be facing not just problems of transition, but a period of prolonged turmoil. Views also differed widely on the importance of international trade issues as sources of instability and conflict among the Western powers.

More of a consensus was reached on the issue of expanding NATO membership to include Central European states – the January 1994 NATO Summit should be tasked with announcing timetables and criteria for membership – whereupon a prolonged pre-entrance phase of extensive contacts should follow; some form of confidence-building agreement would be called for vis-à-vis Russia and Ukraine. Connected with this issue was the question of NATO's mandate and mission. As one Committee member put it, 'the public will not support NATO if it addresses a non-existent Russian threat and nothing else'.

Two issues that were not discussed were the security implications of refugees and population movements, and the long-term US presence in Europe.

The Committee finally moved to establish a list of new research challenges: the relationship between economics and security; area studies with historical and social analysis of conflicts and their roots; the analysis of non-state rather than state actors; and intra-state conflict. The Committee, and the IISS research staff to whom the new research challenges sounded pleasantly familiar, were also reminded of the continuing concern with conflict and violence, however much the perspective on 'new dimensions of security' is widened.

'Democratisation and Norm Creation in Europe' was the subject of Marianne Hanson's paper for Committee 2. This was the Conference on Security and Cooperation in Europe (CSCE) committee of the Annual Conference. The interest in this subject was, it has to be acknowledged, considerably less than in the Committees dealing with Russia, Germany or peacekeeping. This is somewhat embarrassing from a Western perspective because, after all, the West is now facing a liberated Eastern Europe, including Russia, at least partly because the Easterners chose to take the CSCE and its values seriously, to believe in Western models and to act upon this understanding. Today, much attention is focused on the horrors of Yugoslavia, war in the Caucasus and Central Asia. There is rather less attention paid to the long-term effects of the CSCE process, the possibility that the situation in the former Yugoslavia may be misleading us and that under the stormy surface of European conflicts there still runs a strong current of security community-building that may (or will), ultimately, make war on the continent, even in its over-extended CSCE-shape, impossible.

Dr Hanson's paper focused on the crucial fact that the CSCE not only established a set of norms in Europe, but also the idea of accountability and created a procedure for regularly reviewing compliance with the norms agreed upon. These 'intrusive mechanisms' have constituted a revolutionary departure. It might, however, be suggested that much of this was foretold in the UN Charter through its provisions on colonial territories and administration, for which, in the Chapter on the trusteeship system and the accountability of non-self-governing territories, guidelines were given with the provision of information. In this context the UN could be said to be a forerunner of the CSCE.

The Committee discussion concentrated on norms regarding human rights and the rule of law and democracy, with special focus given to the new European democracies and the fact that issues previously considered 'domestic' could no longer be shielded from international scrutiny. 'Europe' was variously identified as both CSCE Europe, the Europe of the Council of Europe and a more narrow Europe of the Community (and European Free Trade Association) countries.

Norms imply standards for accountability and predictability and thus define states in terms of shared values. Norms have a long-term effect. The fact that they are violated from time to time does not 'unmake' the norm. Democratisation, the institutionalisation of freedom, as Professor Frank had stated, has a long-term stabilising effect, although it may bring considerable instability over the shorter term.

Norms that work get no headline attention. Repeated violations, however, will undermine the norm ('when the chips are down, norms do not matter') and there is a certain level of disrespect at which the validity of the norms becomes untenable. Norm enforcement is a problematic issue. Sanctions may have collateral effects, and may actually weaken the democratic opposition in the country targeted, just as much, if not more, as the offending regime. Enforcement may rule out influence. At the same time, decisions will have to be taken with the credibility of the norm system as a whole, and with a long-term time perspective, in mind.

The norms established through the CSCE and the Council of Europe are not enforceable through these institutions – one may talk about 'squeezing states' as a participant chose to phrase his strategy – but in terms of 'power' the CSCE has little to offer. On the other hand, there is every reason to agree with the author of the Committee paper when she stated that the West is now closer than ever to the combination of norms and acceptance.

The Committee also addressed itself to the problem that human rights and norms in general are seen as Western and are really only accepted wholeheartedly by a core of European states. The view was advanced that the EC, rather than the CSCE, is the norm creator. Cultural differences play a role and participants in the debate pointed to the proceedings of the recent human-rights conference in Vienna. A widening of the CSCE framework, and definitions of Europe that would include the Mediterranean shore, would thus present problems. The basic challenge facing CSCE members is, of course, whether 'selectivity' in any cultural or other sense can be applied within that area; either the countries are Europeans or not in terms of CSCE norms.

Committee 3 was assigned the theme 'The Islamic Factor and European Security', but chose to rename itself 'Euro-Security and Neighbours to the South'. Because of the unfortunate illness of the paper-giver, M. Jean-Christophe Victor, the Conference was left without a paper, but is most grateful indeed to Dr Zaki Badawi for speaking at short notice and saving the Committee. In his presentation, Dr Badawi dismantled the myth of a united, armed and determined Islam rising as the enemy of the West, blaming this imagery largely on the media. In focusing on the situation of the Muslims inside Europe – as victims in Bosnia, refugees or immigrants in Western European countries – Badawi also suggested the role that those minorities may play in provoking the rise of aggressive right-wing movements. The danger would thus be one created by the Europeans, causing damage to themselves and to the Muslims, rather than in Muslim extremism *per se*. Generosity in terms of immigration legislation, various aid pro-grammes to Muslim countries on the European periphery and in the handling of the Turkish application to join the EC were recommended.

In the debate in the Committee a number of Islamic risks were identified: political takeovers might happen in countries regarded as 'strategic' by the West; the Americans would say 'Egypt', the Europe-ans 'Algeria'. At the same time, political power acquired through the ballot box might moderate radical Islam. Regional instability might be the result of Islamic political forces operating inside or outside politi-cal structures; terrorism could not be ruled out (although nothing materialised during the Gulf War).

To counter this, Europeans should seek dialogue with radical Islam, pursue economic aid programmes with conditions attached, and pro-mote development in the Maghreb and the Middle East with regional economic and security cooperation in mind. Radical Islam is seen as the form of political opposition available to the malcontent in the Maghreb and Middle East. It is up to Europeans, primarily acting through the EC, to assist in directing this opposition through political channels, within modernising, parliamentary systems.

'Economic and Social Stability – Preconditions for European Secu-rity' was the topic for Laszlo Valki's and Laszlo Csaba's paper in Committee 4. It focused on the situation in the six Eastern and Central European states, ex-satellites of the Soviet Union.

On the basis of economic statistics – declining production, out-of-control inflation, rising unemployment, high debt – the situation is far from encouraging. Furthermore, to the extent that there are 'good figures', as, for example, in the low unemployment figures from the Czech Republic, these really indicate bad news, as they only demon-strate that the country lags behind in closing down its inefficient factories. The only bright spot is the growth in real terms of Polish industrial production during 1992–93. The authors, however, point to two great wonders in Eastern Europe: first, that despite all these difficulties, the six countries are still coping and are worthy of more than an honourable mention in their relative persistence to stick to reform policies. Second, despite declining standards of living there has been no massive dissatisfaction among the populations nor major political disturbances. Parliamentary systems (although with obvious deficiencies) function and the countries keep together and on track. There has been no 'Lebanonisation' or massive use of internal force and inter-state conflict has been contained. In fact, the situation today is more stable than it was a couple of years ago. The fear – one reason behind organising this Committee – that economic failure, social un-

rest and nationalism/irredentism would provide a dangerous conflu-
ence of instability has not been confirmed.

Reviewing the developments in these states shows how perspectives
have changed since 1989. For many years, the liberation of Eastern
Europe was both anticipated and feared because it was seen to carry
the concomitant risk of a Third World War arising in Europe. Now,
Mikhail Gorbachev and his successors have cheated the pessimists on
that one, but far from being grateful for such small graces, the West
now tends to express deep unhappiness when social, economic and
political change does not progress at a speed capable of delivering
immediately democratised, market-adjusted, stable and prosperous
countries in an area of Europe which yesterday was thought as a
potential battlefield.

The debate, in what became known as the 'Budapest Committee',
focused entirely on the six Central European and Balkan states; Russia
and Ukraine were left to other committees. The message of the Committee was one of guarded optimism. There was a certain reaction
against the title that had been given to it as 'stability' was thought to
indicate a Cold War frame of mind on the part of the conference
organisers, while the real issue is, and will remain, dynamic change
and, in the final analysis, economic and social revolution.

As to the speed with which change should be sought an interesting
divide opened with some Nordic participants expressing concern over
the risks that too quick and dramatic change might bring. Instead, a
more managed and cautious track should be followed in order not to
destroy the basic fabric of social cohesion.

It was underlined that what could be described as 'the East' stands
for very different things – economic and social conditions vary greatly
between Slovenia and Ukraine – and that these conditions would also
have very varied security implications in the different countries. There
was general confidence that economic recovery would be attainable
and that in pursuit of this Western, and in particular EC, support would
be helpful. The six Central and Eastern European countries had the
most dangerous years behind them and participants pointed to the
amount of moderation and restraint demonstrated by all six during the
Yugoslav crisis.

There seemed also a general agreement about the relative manage-
ability (if not outright solution) of the minorities issues between the
Visegrad and Balkan states, and that, once these same states found
themselves within the framework of European institutions with the
Community as their safe anchorage, these issues would pose no further
risk at all. Outside worries, including those expressed in the IISS

Strategic Survey 1992–1993 over the Hungarian issue, were criticised with some passion.

In all, the situation in economic, social and political terms was seen to be under control, even though economic stagnation could still cause serious problems. The old Austro-Hungarian dilemma that the situation is desperate, but not serious would seem inadequate; serious, but possibly brightening would be more accurate.

Peacekeeping in Europe is a new phenomenon. The operation in Cyprus was always a relatively peripheral one, and few considered, on a daily basis, that the US presence in Europe was a form of peacekeeping on the most macro-impressive scale. Mats Berdal's paper for Committee 5 focused on the experiences of the former Yugoslavia, the West's continuing trauma of the last two to three years. Dr Berdal posed a set of complex questions: what have been the precise tasks of peacekeeping forces in the former Yugoslavia, and to what extent has the implementation of mandates been influenced by the inability to obtain local consent? What have been the operational consequences of adhering to the established principles and practices of UN peacekeeping operations, and to what extent is the UN equipped to manage large-scale operations in a semi-permissive environment? To what extent can regional organisations effectively complement UN peacekeeping efforts and, in particular, should NATO and its partners become further involved in peacekeeping and even peace-enforcement missions? What are the broader lessons and implications for peacekeeping that emerge from the Yugoslav experience?

The conclusions were phrased in terms of peacekeeping as a substitute for long-term strategy (which it is not!); the limits of political will (which have been embarrassingly apparent – with 'symbolic security gestures' and 'therapy' for television viewers – but little determined action); and the limits of peacekeeping (seen in terms of various organisational, logistic and other shortcomings on the part of the UN itself).

The Committee discussion was structured along two lines: political issues (pertaining to 'will') and operational aspects (pertaining to 'capabilities'). Much of the debate had an admirably academic character – the sound and fury of the Yugoslav crisis and other realities being somewhat distanced from much of the Committee discussion on various types of peacekeeping, peace-making and enforcement. The complications of the 'CNN effect', moral issues and national interests on the part of those states participating in peacekeeping operations were discussed, as was the high premium on early deployment and preventive or pre-emptive peacekeeping. The Lawrence Freedman dictum that intervention should occur on day one (when nobody, of course, realises that intervention is called for) was observed.

The issue of impartiality was discussed, the view being expressed by a representative of a most seasoned peacekeeping country that with the new generation of peacekeeping operations (such as in the former Yugoslavia and Somalia) the era of impartiality was really past. This view was not generally shared, while the question of whether one can be the policeman on the block and still maintain impartiality between the gangs fighting was left hanging in the air.

A considerable amount of the Committee's time was taken up with Russia – on peacekeeping within the former Soviet Union by Russian forces, and the effects upon the international community of peacekeeping being carried out by a single country, and an interested one to boot. The view was advanced, however, that the internationalisation of peacekeeping operations on CIS territory would actually be sought by the Russians themselves – assuming that this would not imply a massive deployment of forces from the major Western military powers. On this there may be different views, however, as Robert Blackwill indicated in his plenary intervention. Several Committee members felt that Russia and its 'near abroad' will constitute the most urgent territory for future peacekeeping operations.

The issue of capabilities was discussed at great length with Berdal's rather merciless treatment of the deficiencies of the UN as its background. Cooperation between the UN and regional organisations was touched on and strong emphasis was given to NATO (plus possibly NACC) as the only credible regional organisation to be a peacekeeping partner and subcontractor. The need for long-term planning and training was underlined. While deployment decisions will have to be taken on an *ad hoc* basis, capabilities could certainly be pre-stocked and certain functions could be achieved in a planned and pre-organised manner.

Committee 6 faced the problems of restructuring military forces in Europe. The paper, prepared by Jacquelyn Davis, provided a discussion both of the changed NATO planning context (also the dilemma of the Western European Union (WEU), ex-Warsaw Pact, ex-neutrals, etc.) and of counter-proliferation planning, on theatre nuclear defences and on cooperative security, a term which in itself suggests a new game altogether (echoes of the Palme Commission!).

The discussion in the Committee centred largely on NATO problems (without much reference, if any, to the WEU). The familiar difficulty now is to determine against whom and what to plan. This makes 'flexibility' a key word and pushes for multipurpose systems, high levels of mobility and versatility. If peacekeeping is the new game, then should existing forces be used on levels 'lower' than those for which they have been designed, or should they be retrained in order to be 'at ease with their role' (which the French Foreign Legion did not think it would be when called upon to undertake a humanitarian task)?

The participants in the Committee debate somewhat simplified the task of the military by suggesting that those who really have to relearn in the new environment are the political decision-makers, who have to know how the new assignments are to be given. The agendas of the various European countries differ – as do, indeed, the agendas of the Americans (much occupied with theatre missile defences and prolif- eration) – and European doubts about the future character of the US engagement and presence in Europe also create difficulties for the Europeans. Uncertainties about possible NATO widening, which was seen in the Committee as posing enormous practical problems, create additional difficulties for force planners over the longer term. Other- wise force planners would be expected to see the present situation as, at least in part, a golden opportunity to design forces from scratch, rather than having to inherit resources not always acquired by design. Rationalisation, as proposed in Dr Davis' paper, is, however, hard to obtain in practical terms, however desirable, given the present general decline in force levels, economic resources and public interest.

Committee 7 discussed 'Russia: Partner or Risk Factor in European Security?' Professor Hannes Adomeit's paper looked first at the vari- ous transformation processes under way in Russia – economic, politi- cal, military and federal – and at their impact on current security policies and concepts; second, at efforts to define Russian identity and national interests on the basis of the interrelationship between these problem areas; third, at the present Russian approach to European security issues; and finally, at the possible future formulation and development of Russian security policies in Europe.

The Committee discussions were divided into four themes: the internal situation in Russia; Russia and the near abroad; Russia and Germany; and Russia and Europe, including the US.

The Adomeit view of internal Russian developments tended in general towards the optimistic. The economic reform process contin- ues, albeit slowly; the political crisis is serious, but still within bounds that may allow for an outcome avoiding a major breakdown; the military supports Yeltsin, is under a measure of political control and has regained professional confidence since last year; general political disintegration is unlikely as centre and periphery still hold together. Russian foreign- and security-policy postures remain within the gen- eral framework of cooperation with the West and are still coloured by overall restraint. It should be remembered that the devolution of the

USSR that has taken place has been largely peaceful and has occurred with a remarkable lack of nationalist and extremist Russian reactions. As decolonisation goes, this is a special case.

In the Committee there were voices expressing scepticism about the Adomeit optimism, identifying greater risks to the economy, the loyalty of the military and the possibility of regional autonomy and restlessness. Still, the view inclined towards the optimistic line – Russia will muddle through with its reforms and will keep together.

However, agreement was also reached that in 1992–93 Russia had changed its foreign-policy orientation in important ways. There is a new assertion of Russian interests in the 'near abroad' and possibly also, most recently, a noticeable orientation towards European priorities rather than the US as a main partner. Russian intervention to maintain stability in Central Asia (Tajikistan) and in the Caucasus (as well as Moldova) reflects selfish interests, but the West is still willing to be tolerant. The Ukrainian problem is different, with the country in deep economic crisis and the continued relationship between itself and Russia a crucial one for both parties, as well as for Europe. For the West, the conflict between the two states presents serious balancing problems: how to provide aid and assistance, especially if, as is now assumed, Ukraine totters on the brink of collapse and refuses to pursue economic reforms.

The relationship with Germany has brought Russia substantial assistance and credits for military relocation and construction, but remarkably little in terms of investments: in 1990, DM 30 million; in 1992 only DM 8m. Comparable figures, for example for Hungary, are far larger.

Western investment in Russia continues, despite a great number of projects (some of which were described in the Committee), to be conducted at a low level or, rather, at a level insufficient for generating capital and resources for rapid take-off. Disillusionment with the West is also apparent in Russia, and all the more difficult to bear when it is realised that the West has been the greatest beneficiary of the collapse of the Soviet Union.

The Committee considered recommendations for what the West might do: working on the micro-economic level supporting regional development programmes; and providing macro-economic stabilisation (inescapable according to some Committee members). Furthermore, the West must also consider how welfare is gradually to reach Russia from Western Europe, how Russia can be integrated, or rather associated, as suggested by Hannes Adomeit, with Western institutions, and, less happily, what the contingency planning should be for a Ukrainian collapse.

Committee 8 discussed Joseph Joffe's paper 'The Role of Germany'. Seen in a historical perspective, Germany has been fated to be a source of instability in both weakness and strength. The Cold Peace since 1945 changed all this, giving divided Germany peace, stability and, in the case of its Western part, unprecedented wealth and prosperity. Bipolarity, 'enclosed in the heart of Europe', provided the setting for Germany's adjustment to a Western European country, integrated in NATO and the EC. With the end of the Cold War and with Germany united, for the first time in its history, says Joffe, it finds itself in an enviable, historically unique strategic position. It has no claims against its neighbours, and they have no claims on Germany. Indeed, for the first time in the annals of unified statehood, Germany is surrounded only by friends. That it is at present beset by the problems brought by unification changes nothing in this picture.

There was consensus in the Committee about Germany's key importance as the European country that will determine the future of NATO and the EC, as the power that will decide the relationship between the West and the countries of Eastern and Central Europe (including Russia) and as the European country that will most strongly influence the role of the US in Europe. German economic growth and the prosperity of a united Germany is desired by all, although this is somewhat tempered by concerns over where the future Germany will go. The possibilities for a new German 'autonomy' outside the European architecture were seen as worrying, although the majority assumed that political and economic developments in Germany over the next two to five years will be generally positive and that the country will master its present problems of cohesion and tendencies towards extremism. It was also expected that Germany would make some headway towards a more active foreign and security policy within existing international institutions and obligations (including peace-keeping operations under the UN Charter). How the Germans might handle the problem of body-bags remained to be seen, however.

Concerning the changed parameters of Joffe's paper – with Germany facing new decisions in a radically changing international environment – there were worries about how Germany would react to major economic setbacks, disturbances in Eastern Europe and, above all, a possible US disengagement from the European continent. The maintenance of the US presence was underlined, it being the only Western power that is not at all afraid of Germany. The German desire for a close relationship with the US made one of the transatlantic participants wonder whether America's function really was to legitimise growing German power, to which the answer from the German side was that 'legitimise' was too strong, but to 'channel' German power was a better way of expressing the problem and its solution. There was also concern on the German side about the possibility of renewed anti-German coalitions in Europe being the possible consequence of a US retreat from the continent.

Committee 9 looked at 'Nordic–Baltic Security'. The Committee was something of a 'family' affair, reflecting the strong Nordic membership of the Institute.

Dr Krister Wahlbäck's paper strongly underlined the particular Nordic situation at the end of the Cold War: despite the revolutionary developments since 1989, very little in the region has changed. The North is different from Central Europe in that Russia, also in its new, weakened state, remains a neighbour, presenting the same fundamental strategic problem to the states in the North as it has done since the end of the Middle Ages. The correlation of forces between Russia and the Nordic states has shifted over the centuries, but Russia has always been there. Today, the three Baltic republics do constitute a barrier of a kind, but it is not in any way comparable to the Central European situation with Russia pushed far to the East – behind the Visegrad countries, Ukraine and Belarus. The Baltic barrier itself presents problems of Russian troop presence, minority issues, economic, social and political uncertainties. The Wahlbäck paper, however, strikes a note of optimism in suggesting possible solutions to the Baltic–Russian security-relations dilemma, indicating a special Nordic role in bridge- and confidence-building and pointing to the possibilities of a region with some 23m Nordics, 8m in the Baltic republics and 15m in what, from the Nordic–Baltic perspective, is 'near Russia'. If this 'near Russia' acquires a real stake in maintaining a cooperative relationship with the Nordic states – also realising old Russian hopes from the 1700s of a window of opportunity, contacts and cooperation with the West – then quite optimistic scenarios could be drawn up for a Nordic–Baltic–Russian future. In the meantime, however, various calamities threaten: unsolved Baltic–Russian issues; illegal immigration; Chernobyl-like accidents; smuggling; and organised crime. However, as Wahlbäck observes, if things go well, the Nordics are better placed than the continentals to make the most of the commercial exchanges with the new Russia. If they go badly, on the other hand, the Nordics would be more exposed.

The debate in the Nordic Committee presented four major themes. First, there was a certain sensation of Nordic loneliness, underlined by the fact that 22 of the 26 participants in the Committee were Nordic. Some members of the Committee, not without justification given the circumstances, felt that little interest is shown in the security situation in the North. As was said by one exasperated participant: 'Only the Russians care about the North!'.

Second, Russia was identified as the main 'problem' with possible scenarios of disintegration or, even worse, the re-establishment of an authoritarian, nationalist and revanchist Russian state. Another scenario, a 'reasonable Russia', could, on the other hand, present a more attractive option.

Third, the situation in the Baltic republics was considered at length, Baltic participants expressing concern both about troop withdrawals and minority issues. Still, a mood of relative optimism prevailed: the overall trend as to withdrawals is positive. It was also noted that Estonian minority policies, the result of CSCE consultation, were more in line with international norms than was suggested by the Western (and Russian) media.

Various forms of security assistance to the Baltic republics were discussed, with the emphasis on internal security (including anti-coups capability) and territorial supervision (frontier, coastguard) rather than an assistance for a military build-up.

Fourth, what is to be done? Here two camps were formed: the activists and the traditionalists. While all agreed on the need not to alarm Russia or to dramatise the Nordic–Baltic security situation, there were clear nuances in terms of how fast and how far the Nordics should go in seeking closer relationships with European institutions. To the traditionalists, the Nordic applications to the EC had their own, discrete momentum (for unaligned Sweden and Finland, the possibilities of future WEU membership and a NATO option are kept open). For the moment, the imperative was to keep links both with continental Europe and with the Atlantic.

Professor Masashi Nishihara's paper for Committee 10, 'European Security in a Wider World', aimed at identifying the role that Europe would still play on the global scene, what impact various security challenges from outside Europe would have upon European security and how the Europeans were to organise themselves to respond to these challenges. This was a heavy assignment and an agenda almost as endless and open as that of Professor Freedman's paper for Committee 1.

Nishihara's paper advances the thesis that Europe has ceased to be the unique continent and region in the world and is now only one of several; it discusses the changes in the international system as a whole, the disengagement from Europe of the superpowers, the global engagement of the new great powers, Japan and China, the so-called Islamic threat, and suggests the 'power' and 'links' approach to handling European security as challenged by the international environment and for the defence of European interests beyond the boundaries of the European continent.

The debate in the Committee focused on three issues: what role should Europe play in support of global security? What assistance do regions outside Europe expect from the Europeans? What European security commitments outside Europe are required for European security?

First, however, the Committee faced serious disagreement about whether Nishihara's thesis about the normalisation of Europe was correct. It was strongly disputed by the commentator, Pierre Lellouche, who still saw Europe as a continent different from others, important in strategic terms and the 'most exposed continent'. Most European participants seemed inclined to rejoice in European normalisation, including the decline of Europe's earlier role as a negative security factor, a cockpit of confrontation, both regional and global.

The second controversy concerned defining Europe, which resulted in an almost infinite variety of definitions. That Europe has to be defined according to function and to the purpose of the inquiry seemed the not-quite satisfactory answer. 'Europe as an idea' offered some consolation. A continuing transatlantic link was assumed by most, and the European defence identity was viewed with considerable scepticism by this group.

As to Europe's role, it was assumed that this would be a matter of choice rather than necessity, that soft security would be Europe's main contribution rather than military force projection. Doubts were expressed about 'Europe', rather than national governments as such, taking action.

The expectations of non-Europeans of the European role in the non-European world were considerably greater than the expectations of the Europeans themselves. The US and Europe were seen by the non-Europeans as joint anchors of global stability and the importance of the continent for norm creation and support was underlined. Aid and assistance were also discussed, although expectations among non-Europeans were that European aid efforts would tend to be concentrated nearer to home. One of the African participants noted that Europe was becoming protectionist to a degree frightening to small countries, while the US at least believed in prospering through the prosperity of others. Europe's non-unified state was underlined by the Europeans themselves, although this was also presented as an asset. In this way there are different horses for different courses: British troops for *Desert Storm*, and Danish aid to the Palestinians.

The importance of the Uruguay Round of the GATT talks was underlined by non-Europeans, less so by the Europeans, whose response to this issue, not as an economic one, but as a vital matter of global security, was rather muted.

In general, in the wide acceptance of European reluctance to assume leadership, recognised by the non-Europeans, there was also an underlying note of concern among Europe's partners. This was, in a sense, all very well, but is a world of regions in which all take such a narrow view of their interests really wanted?

The theme of the 35th Annual Conference of the IISS, 'European Security after the Cold War', is a broad one, and holds more questions and uncertainties than answers. The question mark is not there, but it can be sensed. The title itself is negative: Europeans do not quite know where they are; what they do know is that this is no longer the Cold War. It is also understood that European security is no longer the same as that constant watch over the great balance between East and West which used to be such a preoccupation. Security in Europe is no longer attainable through a frozen status quo upheld by huge military establishments. Europe is out of the trenches and has difficulties in keeping up with change. Truths have to be unlearnt and attitudes to be changed.

The question put to this conference by Sergei Blagovolin, 'are we in this together, are we still enemies or are we somewhere in between?', can be answered in the affirmative. We are in this together, but we do not yet quite know who we all are. Furthermore, we do not quite know what it is that we are in.

Having finally escaped from the great simplifications of the Cold War we are already happily chasing new certainties. Where is the new great theme? John Gaddis has suggested that it is a continuing struggle between forces of integration and disintegration, which does not sound very new, but rather like John Maynard Keynes – 'History is just one damned thing after another'. Samuel Huntington has proposed a scheme of the 'clash of civilisations', of which echoes were heard here and there in this conference. Perhaps, but should we immediately shed our freedom and throw ourselves into a new scheme that explains everything, but perhaps very little? In the 1970s, during the years of the first détente period when the Cold War was thought to be over, we talked about the emerging world society, the global culture, and I remember being exceedingly pleased with myself for devising the formula 'the new hellenism'. Then Muslim fundamentalism, as it was called, overthrew the Shah of Iran and the Second Cold War started in 1979 – so maybe the world culture was not quite there? The clash of civilisations now takes us to the other extreme and elevates Islam to the supreme heights of the next threat and problem. However, it would seem that there is nothing that even the most fundamentalist of Muslims could do that would remotely compare with the damage that the

West seems perfectly ready to inflict upon itself through quarrels over GATT, not upholding peace in Europe, endangering the transatlantic link, or refusing to face up to the necessity for helping and integrating the former East.

As one of the natives, one of course congratulates Admiral Huntington for the discovery of our continent with its historical divisions and rifts – but it is hardly news here. To be a European is to be aware of these faults; to be a European in the Community sense is, I believe, to assume that they can be transcended, and that *political* culture as well as value systems (such as Christianity for example) have been known to bridge so-called 'cultures'. Again, why hastily sell our souls to a new, great explanation when the uncertainties are so apparent about Europe, its boundaries, its major and minor actors, its many fault lines and its possible identity that seems to pass most of our understanding, but which still is there – somewhere?